RECIPES 1·2·3

Fabulous Food

Using Only Three Ingredients

RECIPES 1·2·3

FABULOUS FOOD USING ONLY ❸ INGREDIENTS

Rozanne Gold

Grub Street • London

Published by Grub Street
The Basement, 10 Chivalry Road
London SW11 1HT

First UK impression 1997

Copyright this edition © Grub Street 1997

First published in the United States under
the title *Recipes 1.2.3.* by Rozanne Gold.
Published by arrangement with Viking Penguin,
a division of Penguin Books USA Inc.

Copyright © Rozanne Gold 1996
Photographs copyright © Tom Eckerle 1996

Recipes 1.2.3. is a trademark of Rozanne Gold

Grateful acknowledgement is made for permission
to reprint "Celery" from *Verses from 1929 On* by Ogden Nash.
Copyright 1941 by Ogden Nash.
First appeared in *The Saturday Evening Post*.
By permission of Little, Brown and Company.

A catalogue record for this book is available from the British Library.

ISBN 1 898697 67 1

Printed and bound in Italy by Vallardi

Just a few ingredients, of uncompromising quality,
are all you need to create exquisite recipes.

Acknowledgements

This book is dedicated to my beautiful mother, Marion Gold, who nourishes me with her love.

Heartfelt thanks to Kim Goldstein of Canandaigua/Dunnewood Vineyards; Michele Hunter and Michael Rubin of Rubin-Hunter Communications in Santa Rosa; Lila Gault, Ann Stewart, and Marcy Posner of the William Morris Agency, who have been catalysts for great things in my life.

Special thanks to Judy Rundel and John Sheldon, my wine teachers for many years, who have shared their best vintages, their food and friendship. Judy lent invaluable insights to the "Grapenotes."

More thanks to Chris Styler for helping to test recipes; to Helen Rothstein Kimmel, R.D., for her nutritional wizardry and to Philip Mones, purchasing director of the Rainbow Room, for his extraordinary knowledge of ingredients.

To my editor, Dawn Drzal, may you live happily ever after;

To Fern Berman, my partner in business;

To Michael Whiteman, my partner in life.

Contents

Chapter 1

An Introduction to 1·2·3

•

Alimentary, My Dear: The Components of Taste

When it comes to the senses, less is often more.

So it is with our palates and the way we taste. In addition to our keen sense of smell, the Western vocabulary contains only four descriptors for how we experience a morsel of food: salty, sour, bitter and sweet. The Japanese posit a fifth sensation, called *umami*, a beeflike essence of wild mushrooms.

So when we confront some overwrought dishes that today's chefs bring to the table, we often are not experiencing the layers of flavour we'd like to believe, but rather a muddling or masking of basic flavour components.

A chef adds some lemon juice (an acid) to a dish, then needs to balance it with a base (perhaps cream or butter); but then it becomes bland and needs a herb, or garlic, or sugar; and then some more acid. And so it goes. Recipes elongate into shopping lists.

This realisation led me to develop *Recipes 1-2-3*™, a new repertoire of dishes based on the exquisite preparation of *three simple ingredients* of uncompromising quality—an idea so simple it took decades to come by.

Consider a slow-braising leg of lamb with forty cloves of garlic in a wine-dark broth of Côtes du Rhone: The wine reduces and permeates the meat with heady vapours, while the lamb is transformed from sinewy muscle to spoon-tender richness; the lamb's own fat becomes a kind of self-baster; and copious cloves of garlic not only perfume the meat but also thicken the sauce.

It has been said that taste is 70 percent smell; it also is true that smell stimulates appetite, and that appetite is largely anticipation. The clearly defined aromas seeping from this pot of braising lamb are therefore filling your kitchen with an irresistible kind of culinary foreplay.

Yes, only three ingredients. No, this is not "Minimalist" cuisine.

Taste, a complex realm that transcends the mere ingredients of a dish, plays upon our memories, our cultures, and quite probably on our genes. It takes only a few components of a recipe to trigger a cavalcade of flavours, sensations, and long-lost recollections—and once that is accomplished we should learn that enough is truly enough, that what we've cooked has fulfilled our nutritional and emotional objectives.

In my twenty years as a professional chef, I've imposed dozens of ingredients onto a single dish; used paintbrushes and squeeze bottles to decorate plates; piled food so precariously as to challenge gravity.

Turnabout: Today I'm convinced that we really can create delicious food and orchestrate wonderful meals by combining recipes with just a few ingredients. Perfect for today's cook, these formulations result in dishes that are concentrated in flavour and elemental in taste.

Of course there are other sensory aspects to eating, among them sight, sound, and touch. Surely we feast with our eyes and revel in the sound of clinking glasses. Food always touches our lips, our tongues, and the insides of our mouths, letting us experience the variance of texture and temperature.

And, always, good food touches our hearts.

A Personal Guarantee

I promise you will never think about cooking in the same way again. For me, 1-2-3 has become an intellectual gambol, as well as a satisfying effort to preserve the pleasures of the table.

When I get an idea for a recipe—or see a dish on a menu, or beautiful food in a magazine—I immediately ask myself: What are the elemental flavours? How can I achieve them simply?

Do not misconstrue: The title of this book is not synonymous with fast food, nor exclusively with quick-and-easy. This is not an I-hate-to-cook book.

Recipes using only three ingredients are extraordinarily liberating: The cook can kiss the drudgery of shopping good-bye, and the meal, freed from "ingredient-overload," can now be true to itself. There are always tradeoffs, however.

For example, you may reinvest *some* of that saved shopping time in meticulous attention to dicing, mincing, and julienning—because certain dishes require ingredients of specific size and shape to help define flavour.

Other recipes gain their character by gentle coaxing: slow cooking, oven-roasting, braising, caramelizing—all requiring time to undergo a supernal transformation. This doesn't mean you're implacably tied to the kitchen, for you can weed the garden, hug your spouse or dress for dinner while low heat performs its inevitable magic.

To be sure, many recipes in this book *are* 1-2-3 in terms of both time *and* ingredients. They are "sciue-sciue," or quick-quick in Italian, requiring a flash in the pan, a quick steam bath or seconds in a blender.

Still other recipes focus on simple but artful presentation: a juicy summer tomato, milky-sweet fresh mozzarella, and fragrant basil are so taken for granted that they need to be presented in dramatic ways to make them seem new again.

And there's a bonus: By limiting recipes to three components and by aiming for intense flavour, I've been forced to eliminate extra fat—sometimes *any* fat—which means many of these dishes are surprisingly low in calories.

With the hassles of shopping and the manipulation of many ingredients dramatically minimized, my personal guarantee is that *Recipes 1-2-3* will get you *cooking* again.

Chapter 2

Recipes 1·2·3:
Course by Course

An important goal of this book is to make cooking more user-friendly—without taking any shortcuts.

A second goal is to sweep away the excesses of overly complicated recipes—and thereby to explore a new directness and clarity of flavour that comes from simplicity.

Another goal is to establish more intimate acquaintance with each ingredient—to demonstrate how a roast asparagus stalk differs from one that's steamed; why baked squash makes a different (and better) soup than one that's boiled; how you can cook a voluptuous stew without browning meat in puddles of fat; how you can use one ingredient in several different ways.

A final goal: To prove that you can prepare a three-course dinner for six and still make it through the express lane at your supermarket!

PARTY FOOD AND APPETIZERS

Little Cod Beignets
Cherry Tomato Bonbons
Aubergine on Fire
La Mort du Camembert
Lemony Tahina
Black Hummus
Sherry Vinegar Mushrooms
Extra-Bonus Mushroom Pâté
Cornmeal-Pasta Crisps
Tiny Pepper Cheese Crackers
Party Wraps:
    Vine Leaves and Haloumi
    Radicchio and Smoked Mozzarella
    Pancetta and Boccancini
Lacquered Chicken Wings
Med-Rim Lamb Nuggets, I and II
Angels and Archangels on Horseback
Fried Chickpeas with Sage and Walnut
    Oil
Rosettes of Smoked Salmon on
    Cucumber Rounds
Parmesan Lace Galettes
Ouzo Feta Spread
Wine-Baked Olives
Venetian Wafers
Brillat-Savarin's Fondue
Flying Saucers

Rocket and Mussel Salad, Anchovy Vinaigrette
Farmhouse Cheddar Frittata
Iceberg Hearts, Bacon and Blue Cheese
    Dressing
Swedish Cured Salmon
Bresaola and Asiago "Carpaccio," Truffle
    Oil
Celery Rémoulade, Celeriac Crisps
Roast Red Peppers, Yellow Pepper
    Purée
Veal Sausage with Asparagus Sauce and
    Asparagus Tips
Pan-Roast Oysters with Butter and Leeks
Checkerboard Orzo Salad
Niçoise Socca Crêpe, Marinated Goat
    Cheese
Asparagus and Prosciutto Bundles,
    Melted Fontina
Wild Greens and Blood Orange Salad,
    Orange Vinaigrette
Grilled Shiitake Mushrooms, Garlic
    Essence
Seared Scallops on Sweet Pea Purée
Smoked Salmon "Pitza"
Tomato, Mozzarella and Basil: Six Styles
Salad Frisée with Lardons and Hot
    Vinegar Dressing

FIRST COURSES

Salmon Carpaccio Cooked on a Plate
Salad of Roast Beetroot and Beetroot
    Greens, Walnut Oil
Prawns with a Kiss

SOUPS AND PASTA

Carrot-Ginger Velvet
Port Consommé
"Cream" of Spinach Soup
Fournade: Creamy Chickpea Soup

Soupy Red Beans with Smoked Ham
Avocado Velouté, Fino Sherry
Fennel, Leek and Orzo Soup
Curried Lentil Soup
"Fire and Ice" Gazpacho
Chicken Broth 1-2-3
"Sopa de Salsa"
Yellow Turnip Soubise
Beer and Stilton Soup
Red Wine Onion Soup
An Unusual Borscht: Roast Beetroot,
    Squash and Yogurt
Chilled Cauliflower Crème
Brie and Pear Soup
Ginger Pepperpot, "Glass" Noodles
Sauerkraut "Hangover" Soup
Yellow Pea and Bacon Potage
Veal Tortellini, Turkish Yogurt Sauce
Garlic and Oil Spaghetti
Linguine Riviera, Red Sardine Sauce
Cheese Raviolini, Roast Pumpkin
    Sauce
Hungarian Cabbage and Noodles
Farfalle with Broccoli, Broccoli-Butter
    Sauce
Orecchiette with Chicory and Sun-Dried
    Tomatoes
Angel's Food:
    Angel Hair Pasta with Caviar
    Angel Hair Pasta with Truffle Oil
A Very Old Neapolitan Pasta: Macaroni
    and Tomatoes
Spinach Fettuccine with Tomato Butter
Penne and Pencil Asparagus, Torta di
    Mascarpone

MAIN COURSES

Steamed Clams in Thyme Butter
Barbecue Pepper Prawns
Tuna Burgers, Hoisin and Pickled Ginger
    Root
Red Snapper in Burnt Orange Oil
Crispy Salmon with Pancetta and Sage
Roast Cod with Red Pepper Purée
Rosemary-Infused Swordfish
Pepper-Seared Tuna, Cool Mango Relish
Steamed Halibut, Sweet Pepper Confetti
Salmon Baked in Vine Leaves
Pan-Seared Tuna Niçoise, Tomato
    "Water"
Two-Way Salmon and Courgettes:
    Poached Salmon with Courgettes, Two
        Sauces
    Pan-Seared Salmon, Creamy
        Courgette Sauce
Perfect Chicken Salad
Chicken Roasted in a Salt Crust
Poulet Rôti with Wild Mushrooms
Country-Fried Chicken
Chicken-in-a-Watermelon
Chicken "Villagio," Diced Lemon Sauce
Yogurt Chicken with Blackened Onions
Poussin Under a Brick
Brine-Cured Poussins, Glazed Shallots
    and Parsnip Purée
One Duck, Two Dinners:
    Braised Duck Legs with Apples and
        Sauerkraut
    Sautéed Duck Breasts with Green
        Olives and Sweet Vermouth

Michael's Perfect Roast Turkey with
Lemon and Sage
Roast Veal with Leeks and Rosé Wine
Osso Buco with Tomatoes and Black
Olives
Grilled Veal Chop, Yellow Tomato Coulis,
and Basil Oil
Arista: Roast Loin of Pork with Rosemary
and Garlic
Barbecued Pork Pull
Pork Chops with Vinegar Peppers
Roast Pork Tenderloin with Prunes and
Bay Leaves
Garlic Sausage, Lentils and Diced
Carrots
Calf's Liver with Home-Dried Grapes
Lamb Shanks Alsatian-Style
Lamb Steaks with Tomatoes and Za'atar
Rack of Lamb with Pesto Crumbs
Turkish Lamb Chops
Maple-Glazed Beef Brisket
Coffee and Vinegar Pot Roast
Steak Haché, Cabernet Butter
Pan-Seared Sirloin, Oyster Sauce
Reduction
Mahogany Short Ribs
Fillet of Beef, Gorgonzola Whipped
Potatoes
Prime Ribs of Beef, Horseradish-Rye
Crust

VEGETABLES AND SIDE DISHES

Caramelized Chicory and Bacon
Turnip and Havarti Torte
Fried Lemon and Courgette Salad
Winter Squash and Orange Purée
Turkish Pilaf with Tomato
Watercress Purée
French Beans with Toasted Hazelnuts
Courgette, Black Olive and Tomato
Compote
Whole Roast Garlic with Goat Cheese
Rosemary-Roast Potatoes
Smothered Lettuce with Sumac
Steamed Broccoli, Stir-Fried Pecans
Spoonbread Custard
White Polenta with Parmigiano-Reggiano
Potato-Fennel Mash
Sugar Snaps in Orange Butter
Gratin Dauphinoise
Dry-Curry Sweet Potatoes
Barley-Buttermilk Salad
Bay-Smoked Potatoes
Broccoli di Rape I-II-III
Chardonnay Cabbage
Two-Way Grits:
Cheddar-Pepper
Garlic
Yucca "Hash Browns" with Red Pepper
Creamed Potatoes, Swedish-Style
Wilted Cucumbers, Dill Butter
Wild Rice and Bulgur Toss
Braised Celery Batons, Fried Celery
Leaves
Baked Sweet Fennel, Parmesan Crust

Pan-Grilled Radicchio, Fried Rosemary
French Potato Cake
Giant Glazed Onions, Balsamic Vinegar
Crisp Aubergine Tassels
Oven-Roast Asparagus, Fried Capers
Saffron Orzo
Cumin-Scented Couscous
Aromatic Ginger Rice
Egg Noodles with Butter and Rosemary
Orange and Gold Potato Purée, Sweet
    Potato Crisps
Husk-Roasted Sweetcorn, Chilli Butter
Perfect Mashed Potatoes
Tender White Beans with Tarragon
Ultra Tomatoes:
    Slow-Roasted Plum Tomatoes
    Melted Tomatoes

DESSERTS AND OTHER SWEET THINGS

Green Apple and Lychee Tart
Frozen Maple Soufflé
Dark Chocolate Mousse
Alice B. Toklas's Sugar Candy
Lemon Buttermilk Ice Cream
Strawberries in Grappa
Corsetière's Despair
Pastel Easter Sorbet
Chocolate Bread Pudding
Iced Maple Custard, Warm Maple Syrup
Black Walnut Bars
Chocolate Banana Terrine
Prune Jelly with Prune Kernels
Fresh Blueberries, Lemon Curd Cream

Chocolate Milk Pudding
Chianti Granita
Raspberry Cloud Soufflé
Green Melon Zabaglione
Maple Mousse Parfait
Syrian Shortbread
Bittersweet Cocoa Sorbet
Eggnog and Panettone Bread Pudding
Oven-Roasted Strawberries, Fresh
    Strawberry Sorbet
"Love of Three Oranges":
    Orange Ambrosia
    Marsala Oranges with Toasted Pine
      Nuts
    Orange, Walnut and Pomegranate
      Salad
Cold Rhubarb Soup, Mascarpone
    "Quenelle"
Vanilla Sugar Cigars
Pepper Lime Ice Cream
Fresh Berry "Kir Imperial"
Little Lemons Filled with Lemon Yogurt
    "Gelato"
Chocolate Truffle Torte
"Cannoli" Custard
Strawberry Summer Pudding
Caramelized Pineapple, Black Pepper
    Syrup
Poires Belle-Hélène, Pear Sorbet
Pumpkin Pavé
Yogurt "Coeur à la Crème," Apricot
    Compote
Mille-feuille of Roquefort and Sauternes
Snitz Pie
Almond Brittle from Sicily

Mixed Fruit Rumtopf
Sweet Zwieback
Spoonbread *Pain Perdu*
Sliced Lemon Pie
Granola Fruit Cobbler
Amaretto "Creamsicle" in Frozen
    Oranges
Grapefruit in Campari Syrup,
    Crystallized Grapefruit
Pots de Crème: Chocolat et Vanille
Chutney-Baked Apples, Vanilla Cream
Frozen Hot Chocolate
Hazelnut Tea Cake
Turkish Cherry Bread
Strawberries and Candied Ginger
    Dipped in Chocolate
Cranberry Chutney
Red Wine Apple Sauce

GRACE NOTES

A Note on Salt
A Note on Pepper
My 1-2-3 Pantry Staples

Twice-Baked Oatcakes
Za'atar Pita
Black Olive Tapenade
Garlic Oil
Lemon Vinaigrette
Sweet Mustard Sauce
Herbes de Provence Vinegar
Pickled Greens
Crisp Tortilla Ribbons
Beer Bread
Caraway Cheese Crisps
Labaneh (Yogurt Cheese)
Red Onion Salad
Flavoured Mayonnaises I-II-III
    (Anchovy-Lemon; Sun-Dried Tomato;
    Spicy Coriander)
Yellow Tomato Coulis/Basil Oil
Parsley Juice
Vanilla Sugar/Cinnamon Sugar
Chocolate Maple Syrup
Iced Bedouin Coffee
Flaky Pastry
Strawberry Spoon Fruit
Cinnamon Croûtes

Chapter 3

About the Recipes

Ingredients

Every recipe in this book is based on just three carefully balanced ingredients. Water, salt, and pepper—fundamental to all cooking—are "free."

- *Water* means tap water, or bottled or filtered water if your environment requires it.
- *Salt* can mean table salt; sea salt, coarse and fine; and geographically specific salts, such as French and Italian.
- *Pepper* can mean white or black peppercorns, whole or freshly ground in a mill; and coarse grind or mignonette black pepper, which you can find prepackaged.

Each recipe specifies which types of salt and pepper to use, and when.

Because my recipes are about their ingredients, nothing can mask inferior quality. So you must be willing to trade up a bit, or journey to a speciality-food shop for the very best of what is required.

Few standard supermarket cheeses come close to the singular taste of Parmigiano Reggiano grated by hand as needed; cheap acidic vinegar will ruin a dish that calls for wonderfully mellowed wine vinegar; you dare not substitute margarine for butter or corn oil for honest olive oil without upsetting the balance of a dish—indeed, you may destroy its very validity.

Although we pretend to escape dependency on the seasonal cycles of nature, we delude ourselves. Raspberries shipped from Chile in sealed gas containers in December, broccoli harvested before a frost, tomatoes plucked green and trucked five hundred miles—all are dilute imitations of the real thing that seduce our appetites but corrupt our tastes.

So this book contains a "Calendar of Menus," organized to make the most of products at their seasonal peaks—when, coincidentally, they are cheapest and most flavourful.

In addition, *Recipes 1-2-3* includes serving suggestions, presentation tips, and "add-ons," for free kitchen spirits who want to add a bit more complexity to dishes—and have time to do it.

The 1-2-3 Pantry

"Convenience food" has a pejorative ring; some might call it "shelf indulgence," but my kitchen cabinet is filled with convenience foods!

Thanks to first-rate ingredients, gleaned from around the world, my cupboard brims with maroon sun-dried tomatoes; premium olive oils from Spain, Italy, California, and Israel; jars of coal-black olive purée; Chinese oyster sauce and hoisin sauce; piquant and exotic pomegranate molasses; anchovies and capers coiled in oil, spicy harissa in collapsible tubes, and za'atar—a Middle Eastern spice blend of hyssop, sumac, and sesame seeds.

Convenient? You bet.

I mix granulated sugar with cinnamon, and some with vanilla pods to have quick dessert flavourings right at hand.

My freezer is home to sheets of puff and phyllo pastry, pesto, and pita bread—in case I don't have the time to make my own.

Although we all agree that a long-simmering homemade stock is preferable, some dried products are nonetheless acceptable. I strongly suggest a supply of Chicken Broth 1-2-3 in your freezer, however (page 96).

Late-summer tomatoes make voluptuous sauce, but what about the rest of the year? Pomi brand strained tomatoes and canned Italian plum tomatoes in purée become a better option.

Best of all, many of our new conveniences are of a very high order—flavoured oils (either homemade or bought), roast garlic purée, provocative vinegars such as my Herbes de Provence Vinegar (page 69), exotic styles of mustard, pickles, chutneys, and chayotes—and they facilitate the task of making intensely flavoured dishes that are vivid, rich, and bold.

For the modern cook these ideologically acceptable conveniences induce what I call ISR, or "instant salivary response."

A Note on Salt

All salt is not created equal. Various salts taste different from one another and affect foods accordingly. Table salt has additives (generally dextrose, and tricalcium phosphate to keep granules from sticking); iodized salt has sodium iodide added. Coarser still are sea salts, evaporated from seawater and retaining trace minerals, which in addition to perking up foods impart an appealing crunch when used at the very last minute.

I like French sea salt, and am thrilled when my friend Francesco de'Rogati brings a box of Italian sea salt from his yearly sojourns. French (*gros sel*) and Italian (*sale marino grosso*) sea salts can be used interchangeably.

For *Recipes 1-2-3* use table salt, iodized or not, when the recipe denotes "salt." Use sea salt when the recipe calls for "coarse salt."

It's also fun to experiment with other salts—like Hawaiian alae salt, which is coarse sea salt reddened by Hawaiian clay.

A Note on Pepper

In Britain, pepper mills are filled with whole black peppercorns. In France, they are filled with white.

At home I use both and have two pepper mills near my stove: a large one with black peppercorns and the smaller filled with white. I prefer the assertive taste and pungency of the black peppercorn and use it more often.

White peppercorns have a wonderful camphor-like essence and a unique taste perfect for seasoning specific foods. White pepper is also preferred for cream or butter sauces, or sauces light in colour or texture.

Specific varieties of black pepper are interesting to use. Tellicherry, for example, has spicy sweet heat and a hint of pine.

Both black and white peppercorns are the small dried fruit of an East Indian plant. Black peppercorns are the unripe, sun-dried whole berry. White peppercorns are allowed to ripen completely and are the internal part of the berry.

My 1-2-3 Pantry Staples

Quick and easy recipes that should always be available and ready to use:

Chapter 4

Food and Wine Together

"This wine should be eaten, it is too good to be drunk."
JONATHAN SWIFT

Many of the recipes in this book are for simple foods with complex flavours. I've made a variety of recommendations for food and wine pairings, called "Grapenotes," but the most fun of all is making your own discoveries.

As Culinary Counsellor for Dunnewood Vineyards, I have spent the last few years conducting food-and-wine seminars for distributors, chefs and restaurateurs, consumers, and food and wine writers. It's wonderful to explore the components of taste with unsuspecting subjects who little imagine they will never again taste food and wine together in quite the same way.

Not only do we break every rule in the book—finding wines that taste great with artichokes, preferring a cabernet over a chardonnay with "Seared Salmon on a Moroccan Salad," or discovering how a drizzle of honey on feta cheese will redirect the palate to a particular wine—but we learn several palate-liberating principles:

1. No two people perceive food or wine in identical manner.
2. The *preparation* of a dish is what matters most in matching food with wine.
3. Equally important as matching flavours is matching the weight or body of a particular dish with the body of a particular wine.
4. Our responses to the effects of food with wine are clearly physiological and emotional.
5. The sense of smell is a major player in food and wine pairing. Next comes taste—and all sensory systems connected to it.
6. There may be several different wines, of various colours and characteristics, that will go beautifully with the *same* dish.
7. The marriage of food and wine also speaks to the seasons. While duck braised with turnips and mushrooms is a weighty dish, calling for wines of substance, a spicy chilled Gewürztraminer can make it taste like summer, while a warm Rhône red is more appropriate on blustery days.
8. Your own palate is the only important frame of reference for what works—and what doesn't. Finding out why is a lifelong dialogue with your senses.

I love to ask friends, professional and otherwise, about food and wine combinations that dispel preconceived ideas. My husband enjoys country pâté with an off-dry sauvignon blanc; American food critic Arthur Schwartz is crazy about salty taramasalata and sweet German Spatlese; wine expert Jancis Robinson likes to drink a big white French Burgundy with venison. Others believe that cabernet sauvignon goes with chocolate cake, and I love gamay beaujolais with dense, creamy cheesecake.

Because so many new *types* of wines are flooding the marketplace, it's time to rewrite the old rules anyway. Italians make chardonnay and cabernet sauvignon that taste quite different from what comes from California or France. The French are "deconstructing" their blended wines into separate components, so today you can buy their marsanne, cabernet franc, ugni blanc, or mourvedre.

For good measure, Americans are growing sangiovese and nebbiolo in California, as well as viognier, syrah, and charbono—and conventional wisdom says nothing about how these Old World wines with New World tastes are supposed to link with food.

What goes well with a smoked duck burrito, or Thai-style prawns with galangal and lemongrass, anyway?

If the world is your wine list, then you are your own Christopher Columbus on an uncharted wine-dark sea.

Chapter 5

A Calender of Menus

"If you can capture the season on a plate, then you are the master."
JAPANESE PROVERB

Appetite, properly seduced, has a hard time saying no.

A beautifully orchestrated menu, in harmony with the seasons, is the first step in alerting the senses. For the language of menus is meant to make us hunger.

Playful, enticing-sounding menus can evoke vivid taste memories or trigger sensory responses even before we touch a morsel of food. Each course of a well-balanced menu gently moves the appetite along—from anticipation to satisfaction.

Recipes 1-2-3 features fifty-two menus, one for every week of the year, coordinated with the seasons and linked with time-honoured holidays and celebrations.

In many cases, entire three-course dinner parties can be assembled using only nine to twelve ingredients.

January

New Year's Day Brunch Buffet
Sauerkraut "Hangover" Soup
Swedish Cured Salmon
Creamed Potatoes, Swedish-Style
Flying Saucers
Brillat-Savarin's Fondue
Caramelized Chicory and Bacon
Grapefruit in Campari Syrup,
Crystallized Grapefruit

Italian Family Dinner
Fennel, Leek and Orzo Soup
Chicken "Villagio," Diced Lemon Sauce
White Polenta with Parmigiano-Reggiano
Marsala Oranges with Toasted Pignoli

Dinner Party
Salmon Carpaccio Cooked on a Plate
Rack of Lamb with Pesto Crumbs
Tender White Beans with Tarragon
Baked Sweet Fennel, Parmesan Crust
Chocolate Bread Pudding

Saturday Lunch
Salad Frisée with Lardons and Hot
Vinegar Dressing
Farmhouse Cheddar Frittata
Yucca "Hash Browns" with Red Pepper
Black Walnut Bars

Sunday Supper
Yellow Pea and Bacon Potage
Fillet of Beef, Gorgonzola
Whipped Potatoes
French Beans with Toasted Hazelnuts
Chutney Baked Apples, Vanilla Cream

February

Family Dinner
Iceberg Hearts, Bacon and Blue
Cheese Dressing
Chicken Roasted in a Salt Crust,
Braised Celery Batons, Fried
Celery Leaves
Snitz Pie

Valentine's Day Dinner
Angels and Archangels on Horseback
Prawns with a Kiss
Braised Veal Roast with Leeks
and Rosé Wine
Perfect Mashed Potatoes
Raspberry Cloud Soufflé

Sunday Brunch
Celery Rémoulade, Celeriac Crisps
Roast Cod with Red Pepper Purée
Spoonbread Custard
Sliced Lemon Pie

Dinner Party
Bresaola and Asiago "Carpaccio,"
Truffle Oil

Crispy Salmon with Pancetta and Sage
Potato-Fennel Mash
Slow-Roasted Plum Tomatoes
Bittersweet Cocoa Sorbet
Almond Brittle from Sicily

MARCH

St. Patrick's Day
Beer and Stilton Soup
Maple-Glazed Beef Brisket
Chardonnay Cabbage
Beer Bread
Green Melon Zabaglione

A Mediterranean Dinner Party
Fournade: Creamy Chickpea Soup
Turkish Lamb Chops or Salmon Baked in
Vine Leaves
Turkish Pilaf with Tomato
Fried Lemon and Courgette Salad
Yogurt Coeur à la Crème, Apricot
Compote

An Afternoon Tea
Avocado Velouté, Fino Sherry
Mille-feuille of Roquefort and Sauternes
Wild Greens and Blood Orange Salad,
Orange Vinaigrette
Alice B. Toklas's Sugar Candy

Breakfast in Bed
Orange Ambrosia
Spoonbread *Pain Perdu* with Strawberry
Spoon Fruit

Frozen Hot Chocolate
Cinnamon Croûtes

Family Dinner
Hungarian Cabbage and Noodles
Roast Pork Tenderloin with Prunes and
Bay Leaves
Winter Squash and Orange Purée
Frozen Maple Soufflé

APRIL

April Fools' Day
Cherry Tomato Bonbons
La Mort du Camembert
Chicken-in-a-Watermelon
Garlic Grits
Prune Jelly with Prune Kernels

Springtime Dinner
Salad of Roast Beetroot and Beetroot
Greens, Walnut Oil
"Brine-Cured" Pousins, Glazed Shallots
and Parsnip Purée
Caramelized Pineapple,
Black Pepper Syrup

A Vegetarian Lunch
Roast Red Peppers, Yellow
Pepper Purée
Checkerboard Orzo Salad
Grilled Shiitake Mushrooms,
Garlic Essence
Lemon Buttermilk Ice Cream

April in Paris:
Supper at the Wine Bar
Red Wine Onion Soup
Calf's Liver with Home-Dried Grapes
Gratin Dauphinoise
Pots de Crème: Chocolat

Easter Sunday
Niçoise Socca Crêpe, Marinated
Goat Cheese
Lamb Shanks Alsatian-Style
Melted Tomatoes
Oven-Roasted Asparagus, Fried Capers
Pastel Easter Sorbet

MAY

A May Day Dinner
Asparagus and Prosciutto Bundles,
Melted Fontina
Rosemary-Infused Swordfish
Courgette, Black Olive and
Tomato Compote
Cumin-Scented Couscous
Cold Rhubarb Soup, Mascarpone
"Quenelle"

Birthday Celebration
Brie and Pear Soup
Poached Salmon with Courgettes,
Two Sauces
Watercress Purée and Creamed Potatoes
Oven-Roasted Strawberries, Fresh
Strawberry Sorbet

Dinner from a French Café
Veal Sausage with Asparagus Sauce and
Asparagus Tips
Poulet Rôti with Wild Mushrooms
Egg Noodles with Butter and Rosemary
Dark Chocolate Mousse

Sunday Supper
"Cream" of Spinach Soup
Tiny Pepper Cheese Crackers
Yogurt Chicken with Blackened Onions
Barley-Buttermilk Salad
Turkish Cherry Bread

JUNE

A Weekday Dinner
Spinach Fettuccine with Tomato Butter
Pork Chops with Vinegar Peppers
Rosemary-Roast Potatoes
"Cannoli" Custard

Anniversary Dinner
Barbecue Pepper Prawns
Pan-Seared Sirloin, Oyster Sauce
Reduction
French Potato Cake
Chocolate Banana Terrine

Saturday Lunch in the Garden
Soupy Red Beans with Smoked Ham
Country-Fried Chicken
Celery Rémoulade, Celeriac Crisps
Fresh Blueberries, Lemon Curd Cream
Twice-Baked Oatcakes

Summer Dinner Party
Penne and Pencil Asparagus, Torta di
Mascarpone
Pan-Seared Tuna Niçoise,
Tomato "Water"
Parmesan Lace Galettes
Fresh Berry "Kir Imperial"
Vanilla Sugar "Cigars"

JULY

Mid-Summer Party
Little Cod Beignets
"Fire and Ice" Gazpacho
Pan-Seared Salmon, Creamy
Courgette Sauce
Husk-Roasted Sweetcorn, Chilli Butter
Pepper Lime Ice Cream

Dinner, Trattoria-Style
Crisp Aubergine Tassels
Osso Buco with Tomatoes and
Black Olives
Saffron Orzo
Chianti Granita

Summer Bistro Supper
Seared Scallops on Sweet Pea Purée
Sautéed Duck Breasts with Green Olives
and Sweet Vermouth
Pan-Grilled Radicchio, Fried Rosemary
Pots de Crème: Vanille

A Mezze Sampler
Aubergine on Fire
Lemony Tahina

Ouzo Feta Spread
Black Hummus
Vine Leaves and Haloumi
Za'atar Pita
Med-Rim Lamb Nuggets, I and II
Syrian Shortbread
Iced Bedouin Coffee

AUGUST

Summer Picnic
Tomato, Mozzarella and Basil "Club"
Wine-Baked Olives
Perfect Chicken Salad
Baked Sweet Fennel, Parmesan Crust
Granola Fruit Cobbler

A Special Luncheon
An Unusual Borscht: Roast Beetroot,
Squash and Yogurt
Red Snapper in Burnt Orange Oil
Aromatic Ginger Rice
Wilted Cucumbers, Dill Butter
Fresh Strawberry Sorbet
Sweet Zwieback

A Summer Supper
Rocket and Mussel Salad,
Anchovy Vinaigrette
Orecchiette with Chicory and Sun-
Dried Tomatoes
Amaretto "Creamsicle" in Frozen
Oranges

Family Celebration
Farfalle with Broccoli, Broccoli-
Butter Sauce
Steamed Halibut, Sweet Pepper Confetti
Braised Celery Batons, Fried
Celery Leaves
Strawberry Summer Pudding

Tex-Mex Fest
"Sopa de Salsa"
Crisp Tortilla Ribbons
Pepper-Seared Tuna, Cool Mango Relish
Red Onion Salad
Bittersweet Cocoa Sorbet, Cinnamon-
Sugar "Cigars"

SEPTEMBER

Late Summer Lunch
Steamed Clams in Thyme Butter
Barbecued Pork Pull
Cheddar-Pepper Grits
Giant Glazed Onions, Balsamic Vinegar
Corsetière's Despair

Italian Farmhouse Dinner
Cheese Raviolini, Roast
Pumpkin Sauce
Arista: Roast Loin of Pork with Rosemary
and Garlic
Broccoli di Rape with Anchovy and
Toasted Pignoli
Fresh pears, grapes and Pecorino cheese

Candlelight Supper
Curried Lentil Soup
Grilled Veal Chop, Yellow Tomato Coulis,
and Basil Oil
Slow-Roasted Plum Tomatoes
Perfect Mashed Potatoes
Maple Mousse Parfait

Dining-Light Dinner
Sherry Vinegar Mushrooms
Mushroom Pâté Crostini
Linguine Riviera, Red Sardine Sauce
Little Lemons Filled with Lemon
Yogurt "Gelato"

OCTOBER

Autumn Dinner Party
Veal Tortellini, Turkish Yogurt Sauce
Lamb Steaks with Tomatoes and Za'atar
Smothered Lettuce with Sumac
Black Hummus, served warm
Poires Belle-Hélène, Pear Sorbet

"La Spaghetatta"
Antipasti: Cornmeal-Pasta Crisps
Venetian Wafers
Fried Chickpeas with Sage and
Walnut Oil
Radicchio and Smoked Mozzarella
Pancetta and Boccancini
Garlic and Oil Spaghetti
Broccoli di Rape with Garlic and Oil
A platter of ripe fresh figs

Halloween Supper
Carrot-Ginger Velvet
Mahogany Short Ribs
Orange and Gold Potato Purée, Sweet
Potato Crisps
Chocolate Milk Pudding

Far East Flavours
Lacquered Chicken Wings
Ginger Pepperpot, "Glass" Noodles
Tuna Burgers, Hoisin and Pickled
Ginger Root
Steamed Broccoli, Stir-Fried Pecans
Green Apple and Lychee Tart

NOVEMBER

Italian Regional Dinner
A Very Old Neapolitan Recipe: Macaroni
and Tomatoes
Poussin Under a Brick
Bay-Smoked Potatoes
Broccoli di Rape with White Raisins
Strawberries in Grappa

American Thanksgiving Dinner
Yellow Turnip Soubise
Michael's Perfect Roast Turkey with
Lemon and Sage
Wild Rice and Bulgur Toss
Dry-Curry Sweet Potatoes
Cranberry Chutney
Pumpkin Pavé

Warming Winter Lunch
Steak Haché, Cabernet Butter
Gratin Dauphinoise
Whole Roast Garlic with Goat Cheese
Iced Maple Custard, Warm Maple Syrup

Supper in Your Silk Pyjamas
Smoked Salmon "Pitza"
Angel's Food: Angel Hair Pasta with
Caviar or Truffle Oil
Strawberries and Candied Ginger
Dipped in Chocolate

DECEMBER

A Winter Celebration
Chicken Broth 1-2-3
Coffee and Vinegar Pot Roast
French Potato Cake
Red Wine Apple Sauce
Hazelnut Tea Cake

The Night Before Christmas
Port Consommé
Braised Duck Legs with Apples
and Sauerkraut
Orange, Walnut and Pomegranate Salad
Eggnog and Panettone Bread Pudding

Grand Christmas Dinner

Pan-Roast Oysters with Butter
and Leeks
Prime Ribs of Beef, Horseradish-
Rye Crust
Turnip and Havarti Torte
Sugar Snaps in Orange Butter
Chocolate Truffle Torte

New Year's Eve Open House

Rosettes of Smoked Salmon on
Cucumber Rounds
Chilled Cauliflower Crème, Black Caviar
Garlic Sausage, Lentils, and
Diced Carrots
Mixed Fruit Rumtopf Flambé
Sweet Zwieback

Chapter 6

Party Food
and Appetizers

Party food is snap, crackle, and pop for adults.

Small and savoury, these little morsels resonate with piquancy. They nuzzle our palates. They excite a desire for more. They make us thirst.

Only momentary pacifiers, appetizers are insidious: They appease hunger, then they stimulate it. Again and again.

Such is the life of a wine-baked olive . . . a cherry tomato bonbon . . . an angel on horseback.

Little Cod Beignets

The simplest fish cake you'll ever make, the most ethereal one you'll ever eat. Fresh cod imparts a sweet, meaty taste and a remarkable texture.

ADD-ONS

Throw a handful of curly parsley sprigs (that have been washed and dried) into the hot oil. Fry a few seconds until crisp. Scatter on top of cod fritters. Sprinkle with malt vinegar.

GRAPENOTE

Try with a glass of white Rioja or a crisp fumé blanc.

500 g/1 lb boneless, skinless fresh cod, chilled

2 egg yolks plus 1 egg white, chilled

Peanut oil

Before starting, make sure the fish and eggs are cold. In a food processor, purée the cod until smooth. Add the egg yolks, the egg white, 1 teaspoon salt, and freshly ground white pepper to taste. Process until incorporated. Transfer to a small bowl. Cover and chill 1 hour.

Heat 2.5 cm/1 inch of oil in a heavy frying pan. Drop the cod purée by rounded teaspoonfuls into the hot fat and fry until brown on both sides, about 5 minutes. Drain on kitchen paper and keep warm. Sprinkle with salt and serve hot.

Makes 30

Cherry Tomato Bonbons

Cherry tomatoes attain instant glamour when presented in fancy little paper cups usually reserved for sweets. Guests will delight in these one-bite, pop-in-your-mouth savouries.

2 dozen small-to-medium cherry tomatoes

250 ml/8 fl oz favourite filling:
    Black Olive Tapenade (page 36)
    Lemony Tahina (page 33)
    Aubergine on Fire (page 30)
    Black Hummus (page 35)
    Extra-Bonus Mushroom Pâté (page 38)

15 g/½ oz freshly chopped curly parsley

Wash the tomatoes and remove any stems. Place stem side down on a cutting board. Slice off the top third of each tomato. With a small spoon (an espresso spoon or a melon baller), scoop out the insides of the tomatoes. Sprinkle the insides lightly with salt and turn upside down on a kitchen paper to drain.

Turn right-side-up and fill with desired filling, mounding the filling above the rim of the tomatoes. Chill until ready to serve.

Sprinkle with chopped parsley and place each filled tomato in a colourful 2.5-cm/1-inch paper cup, available at speciality/professional baking shops. Serve on decorative platter.

Serves 6 to 8

ADD-ONS

You can use more than 1 filling for variety.

GRAPENOTE

Serve with a dry white, or viognier from California.

Aubergine on Fire

Harissa, the fiery red relish of Tunisia and North Africa, adds a plea-surable burn to this cool and smoky aubergine dip. Extinguish the flame with crunchy fresh vegetables or wedges of pita bread.

1.25 kg/2½ lb aubergine (2 very large or 4 medium)

2½ teaspoons harissa (see Note)

3 tablespoons light mayonnaise

Preheat the oven to 200°C/400°F/gas 6.

Cook aubergines over an open flame for 2 to 3 minutes on each side until skin is charred and blistered. Place on a baking tray and bake for 40 minutes. Cut the aubergines in half and let them cool. Scoop out the soft pulp and put it in a bowl.

Add the harissa and mayonnaise. Mash well and add salt and pepper to taste. Refrigerate. You can add more harissa if desired, but taste only when aubergine has chilled and flavours have developed.

Makes 425 ml/14 fl oz

ADD-ONS

Add 2 small cloves garlic pushed through a garlic press.

Note: Harissa can be purchased in small tins or tubes from Middle Eastern and some speciality-food stores.

La Mort du Camembert

Here's an ecologically whimsical way to recycle the box in which good Camembert is invariably packaged: the cheese is baked in its own little wooden "coffin."

> 1 (250-g/8-oz) Camembert, including box
>
> Fresh sweet herbs, such as lavender or lemon balm
>
> Sliced apples, pears, or grapes

Preheat the oven to 200°C/400°F/gas 6.

    Peel the wrapping off the cheese. Put the cheese back in the box with a few herbs, cover with the top of the box, and place in the oven. When the cheese begins to melt, remove it from the oven and serve it in the box on a platter surrounded by the fruit.

Serves 4

ADD-ONS

Serve with Twice-Baked Oatcakes (page 32) or thin slices of toasted french bread.

GRAPENOTE

Nice with a California pinot noir, or with a lighter-style French red Burgundy, like Savigny-les-Beaunes.

Twice-Baked Oatcakes

250 g/8 oz rolled oats
125 g/4 oz unsalted butter, at room temperature, plus a little
    for greasing tin
125 ml/4 fl oz sweetened condensed milk

Preheat the oven to 165°C/325°F/gas 3.

Put the oats in a food processor and process until it is the consistency of flour. Put in the bowl of an electric mixer. Add the butter, cut into small pieces, a pinch of salt, and the condensed milk. When well mixed, spread with a flexible metal spatula into a buttered 25x15-cm/10x6-inch tin or in a 24-cm/9½-inch flan tin with a removable bottom.

Bake until slightly brown on top and the dough begins to shrink from the sides, about 25 to 30 minutes. Remove and immediately cut into 16 squares or thin wedges. Reduce temperature to 135°C/275°F/gas 1. When oven has cooled, put pieces on baking tray. Bake 12 minutes or until golden. Let cool. The oatcakes keep well in a tin.

Makes 16 pieces

Lemony Tahina

My version of sesame seed sauce—the condiment of choice in the Middle East—is particularly tart and silken. Use as part of a mezze offering—the Levantine answer to antipasto—or toss with strips of steamed chicken and broccoli florets for a special 1-2-3 recipe.

125 ml/4 fl oz tahini

2 large lemons

1 large clove garlic

Put the sesame seed paste in the bowl of a food processor. Add the grated zest of 1 lemon and 60 ml/2 fl oz freshly squeezed lemon juice. Add the garlic, pushed through a garlic press.

Start processing, and slowly add 80 ml/3 fl oz to 125 ml/4 fl oz cold water until you have a smooth, thick purée.

Remove to a bowl. Add salt and freshly ground black pepper to taste and a little more fresh lemon juice, if you desire.

Makes 250 ml/8 fl oz

ADD-ONS

Serve with Za'atar Pita (page 34) or a basket of crudités for dipping.

Za'atar Pita

The entire old city of Jerusalem smells of za'atar—an intoxicating blend of hyssop, sesame seeds, and sumac. More intriguing than oregano or basil, za'atar is delightful sprinkled on pita and pizza.

4 pita breads
3 tablespoons extra-virgin olive oil, plus extra for drizzling
4 tablespoons za'atar

Preheat the oven to 180°C/350°F/gas 4.

Lay the pita breads on a baking tray. Using a pastry brush, spread the oil evenly to cover tops of the pita bread. Sprinkle each with 1 tablespoon za'atar. Drizzle each pita with a little olive oil. Bake 8 minutes, or until the edges just begin to colour. Let cool and cut in eighths.

Makes 32 pieces

Black Hummus

Intensely perfumed and ominous-looking, this lentil purée reminds me of hummus—and should similarly be scooped up with lots of pita bread. You must use tiny green French lentils (grown in and exported from Le Puy, France) for the proper texture, taste, and colour.

186 g/6 oz French Le Puy lentils

6 tablespoons black olive purée (tapenade)
   (see Note)

1 teaspoon Cognac

Pick over and wash the lentils. Put them in a saucepan and cover with 1 litre/32 fl oz of water. Add 2 teaspoons salt and 12 whole black peppercorns.

Bring to a full boil, reduce heat, cover, and simmer for 35 minutes, or until the lentils are soft. Drain the lentils, saving 180 ml/6 fl oz cooking liquid. Let cool 15 minutes.

Put the lentils in a food processor with the black olive purée. Process until fairly smooth, adding 80 ml/3 fl oz to 125 ml/4 fl oz cooking liquid as needed. Remove to a bowl. Add Cognac, and add salt and pepper if needed. Stir well. Cover and refrigerate.

Makes 600 ml/1 pint

Notes: You can make your own Black Olive Tapenade (page 36) or buy it ready-made.

Black Olive Tapenade

This Provençal-style olive paste has found a permanent place in many home condiment cupboards. Its lusty, assertive taste adds titillation to a variety of foods, from a basket of crudités to a leg of lamb.

> **375 g/12 oz stoned oil-cured black olives**
> **1 (60-g/2-oz) tin anchovies with capers**
> **60 ml/2 fl oz fruity olive oil**

Put the olives and anchovies with capers in a food processor or blender. With the motor running, slowly add the oil until the tapenade is smooth; add an extra tablespoon of oil if necessary. Add freshly ground black pepper to taste.

Makes 300 ml/½ pint

Sherry Vinegar Mushrooms

Slow, gentle cooking and the verve of sherry vinegar are the secrets of this lip-smacking hors d'oeuvre. Stored in the fridge, the mushrooms last for weeks. They won't last for long when brought to room temperature, as there are countless ways to use them.

500 g/1 lb large mushrooms (about 18)

125 ml/4 fl oz olive oil

2 tablespoons sherry vinegar

Cut the stalks off the mushrooms level with the bottom of the cap (leaving the stub of the stalk). Beginning at the edge, peel the mushroom caps with your fingers; save the trimmings and the cut stalks.

Put the mushrooms, stalks up, in a nonstick frying pan large enough to hold them in a single layer. Pour the olive oil over the mushrooms and sprinkle with 1 teaspoon coarse salt. Cover with a round piece of greasepoof paper.

Over a very low flame, heat the mushrooms slowly. Cook 5 minutes, turn mushrooms on the other side, and cook 5 minutes. Continue to cook on each side for 4 to 5 minutes, for a total cooking time of 18 to 20 minutes.

Remove the mushrooms with a slotted spoon. Add the vinegar and 12 whole black peppercorns to the juices in pan. Cook over medium heat 2 to 3 minutes. Pour over the mushrooms. Chill.

Serves 6 to 8

Note: Use the reserved trimmings to make Extra-Bonus Mushroom Pâté (page 38).

ADD-ONS

Add several sprigs of fresh herbs, such as rosemary or thyme, to the pan juices.

GRAPENOTE

Very appealing with a glass of fino or amontillado sherry.

Extra- Bonus Mushroom Pâté

ADD-ONS

To make crostini:
Spread on thin slices
of toasted French
bread as an hors
d'oeuvre or as an
accompaniment to
soup. Also seductive
spread on top of
sautéed medallions
of filet mignon.

This woodsy spread is wonderful slathered on filet mignon before roasting, stuffed under the skin of a chicken, or simply smoothed onto slices of toasted baguette for humble yet delicious crostini.

> **250 g/4 oz mushroom trimmings (peelings and stalks)**
>
> **2 tablespoons olive oil**
>
> **2 small cloves garlic, finely chopped**

Put all the ingredients in a small, heavy pan with a cover. Cook, covered, over low heat for 25 minutes, or until the mushrooms are very soft. Add salt and freshly ground black pepper to taste. Uncover and cook 1 minute.

Purée in a food processor until smooth. Chill.

Makes 125 ml/4 fl oz

Cornmeal-Pasta Crisps

More interesting than potato crisps, more addictive than popcorn, these too go crackle and crunch. Try them with as many different pasta shapes as you please. Radiatore ("little radiators") are especially habit-forming, if you can find them.

250 g/½ lb farfalle (bowtie) pasta or radiatore

50 g/2 oz yellow cornmeal (polenta)

Vegetable oil

Bring salted water to a boil in a large pan. Add the pasta and cook until tender, about 12 minutes. Drain well and pat each piece dry.

In a bowl, mix the cornmeal with ¾ teaspoon salt and freshly ground black pepper. Toss the pasta thoroughly with the cornmeal mixture.

Heat 6 mm/¼ inch oil in a nonstick frying pan. Add the pasta, making sure the pieces don't overlap, and fry 1 to 2 minutes on each side, until crisp and just beginning to get golden brown. Serve warm, sprinkled with additional salt.

Makes one good-size bowlful

ADD-ONS

Sprinkle warm pasta crisps with grated Parmesan cheese or your favourite spice mixture.

Tiny Pepper Cheese Crackers

On twenty minutes' notice, you can have warm and elegant snacks for friends who drop in. These bracing little bites marry well with a host of thirst quenchers, from iced tea to ice-cold beer.

50 g/2 oz plus 3 tablespoons grated Parmigiano-Reggiano cheese

125 g/4 oz unsalted butter, at room temperature

155 g/5 oz sifted flour

With an electric mixer, cream together 50 g/2 oz of the grated cheese and the butter. Mix the flour together with 1 teaspoon salt and 1 teaspoon coarse ground black pepper. Add to the creamed mixture and blend.

Form into balls 12 mm/½ inch in diameter, flatten slightly with your palm, and place on an ungreased baking sheet. Sprinkle with remaining cheese. Chill 30 minutes.

Preheat the oven to 230°/450°F/gas 8. Bake the crackers 13 to 14 minutes, until lightly browned.

Makes 30 bite-size crackers

ADD-ONS

Fold 90 g/3 oz finely chopped pecans into the dough.

GRAPENOTES

Also nice with a glass of chilled sweet vermouth with a lemon twist.

Party Wraps

These attractive little roll-ups pack a flavour wallop in just a few bites. The combinations have been carefully matched for maximum contrast of flavour and texture: bitter radicchio and smoky mozzarella; briny vine leaves and pungent haloumi (a white goat's-milk cheese from Cyprus often flavoured with a touch of mint); crisped pancetta and soft boccancini (little mouthfuls of fresh mozzarella). Serve one variety—or a grand platter of them all.

Vine Leaves and Haloumi

> **12 large vine leaves, packed in brine**
>
> **250 g/8 oz haloumi cheese, in one piece (see Note)**
>
> **60 ml/2 fl oz olive oil**

Separate the vine leaves and pat each one dry. Cut the cheese into rectangles 10 mm/⅓ inch thick by 5 cm/2 inches long by 2.5 cm/1 inch wide.

Cut the vine leaves in half from top to stalk. Wrap the cheese pieces in the leaves, folding the sides over like an envelope and rolling to cover.

Heat the oil in a nonstick frying pan. Sauté the "wraps" on each side until cheese just begins to melt. Place on a platter. Serve warm.

Makes 24 pieces

Note: You can substitute kasseri or firm feta cheese if haloumi is not available.

Radicchio and Smoked Mozzarella

1 large head radicchio

250-g/8-oz piece smoked mozzarella

60 ml/2 fl oz olive oil

ADD-ONS

Serve with wedges of lemon.

Bring salted water to a boil in a large pan. Remove the core from the radicchio and remove any brownish outside leaves. Carefully separate leaves. Place the radicchio in boiling water and cook for 3 to 4 minutes. Put the leaves under cold running water in colander until they cool.

Pat each leaf very dry. Cut the mozzarella into rectangles that are 10 mm/⅓ inch thick by 5 cm/2 inches long by 2.5 cm/1 inch wide.

Wrap the cheese pieces in radicchio leaves, folding the sides over like an envelope and rolling like a cigar. They will look like stuffed vine leaves.

Heat the oil in a nonstick frying pan. Sauté the wraps on each side until the cheese just begins to melt. Place on a platter. Sprinkle with coarse salt and serve warm.

Makes 20 to 24 pieces

Pancetta and Boccancini

250 g/8 oz pancetta, very thinly sliced

500g/1 lb mozzarella cheese or boccancini
(see Note)

12 large fresh basil leaves, cut in half
lengthwise

If the slices of pancetta are large, cut them in half. Using a 2.5-cm/
1-inch melon baller, scoop out the mozzarella cheese, or use bought
boccancini.

Wrap a basil leaf around each cheese ball and wrap a slice of
pancetta around the basil. Secure with a cocktail stick or wooden
skewer that has been soaked in water for 30 minutes.

Preheat the grill. Put wraps on the grill pan and grill 3 to
4 minutes on each side, until pancetta is crisp. Serve hot.

Makes 18

Note: Boccancini are small "mouthfuls" of mozzarella cheese formed into balls
approximately 2 cm/¾ inch in diameter.

Lacquered Chicken Wings

ADD-ONS

Sprinkle with rice vinegar before serving. Or scatter toasted sesame seeds on top.

GRAPENOTE

How about sake on ice with a long, thin strip of cucumber?

Incredibly good but oh, so sticky; you might consider finger bowls for your guests. Slow baking creates a mahogany glaze, sealing in the sweet and salty flavours that characterize much of Oriental cookery.

12 large chicken wings

125 ml/4 fl oz dark soy sauce

125 g/4 oz dark soft brown sugar

Preheat the oven to 180°C/350°F/gas 4.

Cut off the wing tips with a sharp, heavy knife and discard. Cut wings into two pieces, separating them at the joint.

Place the wings in a shallow roasting tin. Combine the soy sauce and sugar and a liberal grinding of black pepper and pour the mixture over the chicken, coating it well. Let marinate 30 minutes.

Bake for 30 minutes. Remove the tin from the oven and turn each piece with tongs. (For a more elegant look, transfer wings to a wire rack at this point in the recipe.) Bake an additional 30 minutes. Turn again and bake 15 minutes longer. The wings will be a rich dark brown and very tender. Serve on a platter.

Makes 24 pieces

Med-Rim Lamb Nuggets, I and II

In Arabic cultures these aromatic nuggets would be known as kefta: a mixture of minced lamb (or beef) with spices and flavourings, formed into balls, sausages, or long, thin "snakes." On skewers, they're called kefta kebabs.

I.

250 g/8 oz minced lamb

1 large clove garlic, pushed through a garlic press

½ teaspoon ground cumin

II.

250 g/8 oz minced lamb

½ tablespoon dried mint

2 tablespoons freshly chopped onion

Put the minced lamb, the spices of your choice, 1 tablespoon cold water, ½ teaspoon salt and freshly ground black pepper in a medium bowl. Mix well with your hands. Roll between your palms to make oval shapes 3 cm/1¼ inches long by 2 cm/¾ inch wide.

Preheat the grill. Place the lamb nuggets on a baking tray and grill 5 minutes. Serve hot.

I, II: Makes 14 to 15 nuggets for 250 g/8 oz of lamb

ADD-ONS

You can insert a wooden skewer into each nugget length-wise. Good with tomato-za'atar sauce (page 164).

GRAPENOTE

Experiment with a medium-weight merlot from California.

Angels and Archangels on Horseback

Often used as a "savoury" in traditional menus, Angels on Horseback are served at the end of the meal, after the sweet, to neutralize the sugar taste before port is served. When scallops are substituted, the dish is known as Archangels on Horseback. (Archangels are angels of particularly high rank.) They also make great party food.

6 to 8 slices of brioche loaf or thin white bread, crusts removed

2 dozen fresh oysters or large scallops

12 slices of bacon

Preheat the oven to 230°C/450°/gas 8.

Cut 4-cm/1½-inch circles out of the bread; you should have 24. Toast lightly on both sides in the oven (about 7 minutes total). Reserve.

Pat the oysters or scallops dry with kitchen paper.

Cut the bacon strips in half and wrap each strip around an oyster or scallop. Secure tightly with cocktail sticks.

Place in a baking tin. Bake the oysters for 10 minutes, scallops for 12 minutes. Remove the cocktail sticks and serve on the toasts.

Makes 24

ADD-ONS

You can spread the warm toasts with anchovy paste. A whole flat parsley leaf looks splendid on each scallop.

GRAPENOTE

These heavenly morsels call for a good brut Champagne.

Fried Chickpeas with Sage and Walnut Oil

This is my husband's favourite party food, but he likes these equally well strewn over a piece of char-grilled swordfish. We first tried these crunchy beans with crisp bits of fried sage somewhere near Frontière—where Italy meets France. Use freshly cooked chickpeas for the best texture.

250 g/8 oz cooked chickpeas (see Note)

3 tablespoons walnut oil

1½ tablespoons dried sage leaves (see Note)

Use freshly cooked or canned chickpeas. Drain well and pat completely dry.

In a medium-size nonstick frying pan, heat the oil. When the oil is hot but not smoking, add the chickpeas and fry until they get crisp (they should be crisp on the outside, creamy on the inside). Add the sage leaves and ½ teaspoon coarse salt. Continue to cook 1 to 2 minutes. Drizzle with a little more walnut oil if the chickpeas look dry.

Let cool a few minutes before serving with drinks. Provide lots of napkins.

To serve as a side dish, add a few tablespoons of water and simmer, covered, 2 minutes. Drizzle with a little walnut oil.

Serves 6

Notes: To cook chickpeas: Soak 250 g/8 oz overnight in cold water. Drain, cover with water, and cook about 2 hours, or until tender.

You can buy whole dried sage leaves in speciality-food shops, Middle Eastern shops, or spice shops.

Rosettes of Smoked Salmon on Cucumber Rounds

ADD-ONS

Put a sprig of fresh dill in the centre of each rosette. Serve on a bed of thinly sliced lemons.

GRAPENOTE

Serve with a salmon-hued rosé champagne—a Billecart-Salmon, perhaps?

One of the most popular hors d'oeuvre at the Rainbow Room restaurant in New York, these roses are elegant and edible. Use a young cucumber for a seedless and uniform base. Serve on a crystal platter garnished with garden-variety roses—salmon-coloured, of course.

**1 cucumber (long and thin, about 4 cm/
1½ inches in diameter)**

250 g/8 oz very thinly sliced smoked salmon

125 g/4 oz softened cream cheese

Wash the cucumber. Do not peel. Cut into thin circles, 6 mm/¼ inch thick, and pat dry. There should be about 24 slices.

Slice the smoked salmon into strips 2.5 cm/1 inch wide by 7.5 cm/ 3 inches long, making about 24 pieces. Roll loosely. Curl back the edges and flatten slightly so that it begins to look like a rose. Spread about 1 teaspoon of cream cheese on each cucumber slice and place rosette on top.

If desired, fill the centre of each "rosette" with about ½ teaspoon cream cheese. Arrange on a platter.

Makes 24

Parmesan Lace Galettes

These miraculous, delicate disks are simply fashioned from melted cheese. Delicious warm or at room temperature, they stay crisp and translucent. If you want to feel like a three-star chef, garnish salads and fish dishes with a galette. In Italy these are known as frico croccante.

60 g/2 oz unsalted butter

125 g/4 oz grated good-quality Parmesan cheese

2 teaspoons fennel seeds, cumin seeds, or caraway seeds

In a 20-cm/8-inch nonstick frying pan, melt 7 g/¼ oz of the butter over low heat. Let it get foamy but not brown.

Coat the bottom of the frying pan with 30 g/1 oz of the grated cheese. Sprinkle evenly with ½ teaspoon fennel, cumin, or caraway seeds. Pack down with a metal spatula and let the cheese melt slowly and begin to brown and harden. Flip the galette over, adding 7 g/¼ oz butter to pan. Let the cheese get golden brown on other side. This will take about 4 to 5 minutes on the first side, 2 to 3 minutes on the second side. The galette will be crisp. Remove the galette from the frying pan to kitchen paper. Repeat the process three more times, using the same amounts of butter and cheese.

Serve warm with cocktails, or as a dramatic garnish for main courses and salads.

Makes 4 galettes, 15 cm/6 inches in diameter

Ouzo Feta Spread

"Mezedes," little dishes of food customarily served with drinks, form the basis of social life in Greece. They are served in neighbourhood "ouzeries"—pubs that feature ouzo (a clear, fiery, licorice-flavoured alcohol) and appetizers such as this one.

ADD-ONS

Serve with warm pita bread or Flying Saucers (page 55) and fresh cucumber spears.

375 g/12 oz feta cheese, in one piece

3 tablespoons extra-virgin olive oil

1 tablespoon ouzo (see Note)

Soak the block of feta in a bowl with cold water to cover for 30 minutes. Remove from the water and pat dry.

Crumble the cheese into the bowl of a food processor. Begin to process the cheese and slowly add the olive oil. Blend until completely smooth. Add the ouzo and some freshly ground black pepper. Process until incorporated.

Chill 2 hours. Drizzle with a little olive oil before serving.

Makes 375 ml/12 fl oz

Note: You can use another licorice-flavoured liqueur, such as anisette, sambuca, or pernod.

Wine-Baked Olives

For wine enthusiasts who think "life is a cabernet," here's a creative use for bottom-of-the-bottle leftovers. Baked in rich red wine, olives become fleshy and voluptuous.

    500 g/1 lb kalamata olives

    125 ml/4 fl oz dry red wine (a cabernet)

    60 ml/2 fl oz extra-virgin olive oil or Garlic Oil
        (page 52)

Preheat the oven to 180°C/350°F/gas 4.

    Put the olives in a small saucepan and cover with water. Bring to a boil and boil for 1 minute. Drain well in a colander.

    In a small ovenproof, non-metallic dish, put olives, wine, and olive oil or Garlic Oil.

    Bake 30 minutes, turning once during baking. Serve warm or at room temperature. Much of the liquid will have evaporated.

Makes 500 g/1 lb (about 85)

Garlic Oil

16 medium-to-large cloves garlic
500 ml/ 16 fl oz olive oil
2 fresh bay leaves

Peel the garlic and place in oil in small, heavy enamel pan. Heat gently 5 minutes, or until bubbles form on top. Turn off heat. Add the bay leaves and ½ teaspoon whole black peppercorns. Let steep and let cool. The garlic oil will last two weeks in the refrigerator.

Makes 500 ml/ 16 fl oz

THE FOLLOWING PHOTOS DEPICT:

Party Food and Appetizers:

1. Cherry Tomato Bonbons
2. Party Wraps:
   Radicchio and Smoked Mozzarella
   Vine Leaves and Haloumi
3. Rosettes of Smoked Salmon on Cucumber Rounds
4. Lacquered Chicken Wings

First Courses:

5. Prawns with a Kiss
6. Celery Rémoulade, Celeriac Crisps, Roast Red Peppers,
   Yellow Pepper Purée; Salad of Roast Beetroot and Beetroot Greens, Walnut Oil
7. Seared Scallops on Sweet Pea Purée
8. Tomato, Mozzarella and Basil: Six Styles

Venetian Wafers

A crisp, flavourful snack to accompany a glass of sparkling wine, this is a quick study of textural contrasts: cold bubbles cut through warm richness. Dream of the Piazza San Marco and the Grand Canal.

24 slices sopressata salami, 7.5 cm/3 inches in diameter

60 g/2 oz grated good-quality Parmesan cheese

2 tablespoons fennel seeds

Preheat the oven to 260°C/500°F/gas 9.

Place sopressata on a large baking tray. Put 1 teaspoon cheese on top of each slice of sopressata to cover evenly. Sprinkle each with fennel.

Bake 5 minutes. Remove from the oven and serve while still warm. Wafers will be crisp.

Makes 24 wafers

GRAPENOTE

Drink a glass of chilled prosecco, the dry sparkling wine of the Veneto region.

Brillat-Savarin's Fondue

ADD-ONS

Serve with slices of a good-quality baguette, lightly toasted, rubbed with a garlic clove. Grilled Shiitake Mushrooms, Garlic Essence (page 76), go well with this fondue and together make an exciting meal.

GRAPENOTE

"Call for the best wine, which will be copiously drunk, and you will see miracles." Quote is from M.F.K. Fisher's adaptation of Brillat-Savarin's *The Physiology of Taste*, 1986.

Not like any fondue you've had before, this version offered by the revered gastronome Anthelme Brillat-Savarin in The Physiology of Taste *(1825) is somewhere between molten cheese sauce and soft scrambled eggs.*

His recipe went like this: "Weigh the number of eggs you wish to use, according to the presumed number of your guests. Then take a piece of good Gruyère cheese weighing one-third of this amount, and a morsel of butter weighing one-sixth of it." My version follows.

6 eggs

125 g/4 oz Gruyère cheese

60 g/2 oz unsalted butter, plus additional butter for coating casserole

Beat the eggs well. Cut the cheese and butter in small cubes. Pour all into a buttered flameproof casserole or a buttered 30-cm/12-inch oval gratin dish.

"Put the casserole on a lively fire, and turn the contents with a spatula, until they have become properly thick and soft; add a little salt, or none at all according to whether the cheese is old or not, and a good amount of pepper, which is one of the characteristics of this time-honoured dish; serve it on a gently heated platter."

Serves 4

Flying Saucers

Serendipity in the kitchen led to this amazing transformation of flour and oil into light, fluffy Frisbees of fried bread served hot from the frying pan.

155 g/5 oz sifted flour

2 tablespoons plus 60 ml/2 fl oz olive oil

2 spring onions, trimmed and sliced thin

Sift together the flour and ½ teaspoon salt. Put the flour mixture in the bowl of an electric mixer. Make a well in the centre and add 60 ml/2 fl oz warm water and the 2 tablespoons olive oil. With the dough hook, mix until a dough forms and knead 6 to 7 minutes, until dough is smooth and satiny.

Add the spring onions and mix for just a few seconds longer; over-mixing will make the dough sticky.

Divide the dough into 4 balls. Roll out each on a lightly floured surface to a diameter of 15 cm/6 inches and a thickness of 6 mm/¼ inch.

(You can roll the pancakes out as long as 3 hours prior to cooking, separating them with kitchen paper and then wrapping the stack in cling film.)

Heat the remaining oil in a 20-cm/8-inch frying pan and fry the circles of dough, one at a time, until golden brown on both sides. Keep them warm while you finish making all of them. Cut into triangles and serve immediately.

Serves 8

ADD-ONS

For an interesting first course, place a mound of julienned rocket on top of each flying saucer. Drizzle with Lemon Vinaigrette (page 56) and a dash of freshly ground black pepper. Serve with a fork and knife.

GRAPENOTE

Serve with a chilled California riesling. Or try an Alsatian pinot blanc from Leon Beyer or Pierre Sparr.

Lemon Vinaigrette

A lovely and refreshing splash for green salads mixed with lots of herbs and tossed with freshly cooked legumes (white beans or trendy borlotti, or cranberry, beans) or steamed vegetables (carrots, broccoli, leaves of Brussels sprouts).

1 teaspoon Dijon mustard
3 tablespoons fresh lemon juice
125 ml/4 fl oz extra-virgin olive oil

Whisk together the mustard and the lemon juice. Slowly whisk in the olive oil, a little at a time, until emulsified. Season with ½ teaspoon coarse salt and freshly ground white pepper.

Makes 150 ml/5 fl oz

Chapter 7

First Courses

The notion of a first course has changed over the years.

What once were the first-course mandates—grapefruit maraschino, or prawn cocktail—have given way to anarchy-on-a-plate: nachos grandes, foie gras nuggets, and main-courses-in-miniature.

However difficult they may be to define today, many of us opt for two or three and call it dinner.

Salmon Carpaccio Cooked on a Plate

ADD-ONS

Sprinkle some fresh
lemon juice over the
top.

*Gerard Pangaud, chef at Restaurant Aurora in New York, gained fame
in Paris for cooking food directly on a dinner plate placed in an ultra-
hot oven. This "flash-heat" method produces the most natural tastes and
satiny textures. Be sure to use a heat-resistant plate!*

**500-g/1-lb piece fresh salmon fillet, cut from
the centre of the fish**

**2 tablespoons green peppercorns, drained
(see Note)**

Extra-virgin olive oil

GRAPENOTE

Open a bottle of
buttery chardonnay.
Or try a vintage Krug
champagne with
some bottle age.

Remove the skin and with tweezers remove all the little bones from
the salmon. Freeze 15 minutes, or until very cold. This will make it
easier to slice.

Slice the salmon very thin on an extreme angle, as if it were
smoked salmon. Put the slices between sheets of greaseproof paper
and press down with the heel of your hand to flatten.

Preheat the oven to 260°C/500°F/gas 9.

Arrange the slices in one layer, not overlapping, to cover the
surface of six 23-cm/9-inch ovenproof plates. Season with a little
coarse salt, freshly ground white pepper, 1 teaspoon green peppercorns, and several teaspoons of oil. Let sit 15 minutes.

Put the plates in the oven for 2 to 3 minutes to warm the salmon,
but do not let it cook through. Serve immediately, handling the plates
with a oven mit.

Serves 6

Note: Green peppercorns come in small tins, packed in brine, available in supermarkets
and speciality-food shops.

Salad of Roast Beetroot and Beetroot Greens, Walnut Oil

How considerate of the beetroot to provide two vegetables in one, edible leaves and a thick, fleshy root. This gorgeous salad is enhanced by the sophisticated coupling of walnut oil and fresh lemon. Pass the pepper mill and some warm bread rolls.

> **2 bunches of medium-to-large fresh beetroot, with beetroot tops**
>
> **80 ml/3 fl oz walnut oil**
>
> **3 tablespoons fresh lemon juice**

Preheat the oven to 200°C/400°/gas 6.

Cut the leafy greens off the beetroot and save them. Trim and wash the beetroot but do not peel them. Put them in a shallow casserole with 6 mm/¼ inch of water and bake 1½ hours. Add a little more water during baking. When the beetroot are tender, a knife will penetrate them easily; remove from the oven and let cool. Peel with a sharp knife. Cut the beetroot into 4 cm- by 6-mm/1½- by ¼-inch batons.

Put the beetroot in a bowl and toss with 1 tablespoon walnut oil and 1 tablespoon lemon juice. Sprinkle with salt. Keep at room temperature.

Bring a large pan of salted water to a boil. Wash the beetroot greens well and break them into large pieces. Add the greens to the pan and cook 5 minutes, or until tender.

Drain well. Let cool and toss with remaining walnut oil and lemon juice. Add salt and freshly ground black pepper to taste. Serve greens on a platter, scattered with cooked beetroot "batons."

Serves 4 to 6

Top with warm freshly cooked bacon that is barely crisp and coarsely crumbled. Or add walnuts that have been lightly toasted.

GRAPENOTE

Because there is a minimum of acid, this salad does nicely with wine. Try a chenin blanc or semillon, or a fruity rosé.

Prawns with a Kiss

When you suck the tender meat from these crusty crustacean shells, you make wonderful little noises that sound like slurpy kisses. "Col bacio" in Italian, this dish was inspired by Marcella Hazan.

ADD-ONS

Serve with lemon wedges and an abundance of paper napkins.

GRAPENOTE

This dish requires a bold white of considerable heft, like a chardonnay.

1 kg/2 lb large prawns in their shells

75 g/2½ oz dry bread crumbs

**150 ml/ 5 fl oz Garlic Oil (page 52) plus extra
for drizzling**

Pat prawns dry. Leave the shells intact but remove the small legs with scissors. If using smaller prawns, slip a cocktail stick under the shells running the length of the prawns to keep them straight.

Put the prawns in a bowl with 160 ml/ 5 fl oz of the oil, and a liberal amount of coarse salt and coarse ground black pepper. Marinate at room temperature for 1 hour.

Preheat the grill. Toss the prawns with the bread crumbs, place in a shallow baking tin and grill close to the heat for 1 to 2 minutes on each side. Shells will be slightly charred. Sprinkle with additional coarse salt and drizzle with 2 tablespoons garlic oil.

Serves 6

Rocket and Mussel Salad, Anchovy Vinaigrette

This dish tastes and smells of the deep blue sea. "Liquor" from the mussels softens the anchovies' intensity, while rocket adds a refreshing peppery note. Use plump green-lipped mussels from New Zealand if you can find them.

500 g/1 lb fresh medium-size cultivated mussels in shells

2 large bunches rocket

1 (60-g/2-oz) tin anchovies with capers

Wash the mussels well in a colander. Remove the beards if necessary. Do not dry the mussels. Transfer them to a heavy pan. Add 60 ml/ 2 fl oz water, cover the pan tightly, and cook over low heat, shaking the pan occasionally. The mussels will open in 3 to 4 minutes. Remove from the heat, uncover, and let the mussels cool. Remove the mussels from their shells and reserve the cooking liquid.

Thoroughly wash the rocket. Dry well and keep chilled.

Put the anchovies with capers and the oil from the tin in a blender and purée until smooth. Add 2 to 3 tablespoons mussel liquid and some freshly ground black pepper. Toss the rocket with the cooled mussels. Pour just enough dressing over the salad to coat the leaves lightly, and toss.

Serves 4

ADD-ONS

Add 2 teaspoons balsamic vinegar to the blender, or pass a cruet of vinegar at the table. Colourful and delicious with wedges of hard-boiled eggs.

GRAPENOTE

Try a chenin blanc from the Loire Valley or a more earthy Gavi, from Italy.

Farmhouse Cheddar Frittata

Thick, flat omelettes served hot or at room temperature can be found in Spain as tortillas *and in Italy as* frittate. *Hybrid flavours like sharp farmhouse Cheddar and spicy, pickled jalapeños make this preparation decidedly global.*

375 g/12 oz farmhouse Cheddar

60 g/2 oz sliced pickled jalapeño peppers from a jar, reserving 2 tablespoons liquid

10 extra-large eggs

Preheat the oven to 180°C/350°F/gas 4.

Grate the cheese on the largest holes of a hand grater. Reserve.

Pat the jalapeño slices dry with kitchen paper. Spray a 25-cm/10-inch springform tin with a removable bottom with vegetable oil spray. Scatter the jalapeños evenly on the bottom of the tin. Sprinkle the cheese evenly on top.

Put the eggs, ½ teaspoon salt, and a pinch of white pepper in the bowl of an electric mixer. Mix on medium speed for 4 minutes, or until very light. Add the 2 tablespoons reserved juice and mix.

Pour the eggs over the cheese in the tin. Place the tin on a baking tray and bake for 20 to 25 minutes. Let cool 10 minutes before serving.

Serves 6 to 8 as a first course, 16 as hors d'oeuvre

ADD-ONS

Serve with Roast Red Peppers, Yellow Pepper Purée (page 68), for a delightful lunch. Or serve a smaller portion, garnished with a tuft of wild greens dressed with a simple vinaigrette, as a first course.

GRAPENOTE

I like beer with this, particularly Belgian beer.

Iceberg Hearts, Bacon and Blue Cheese Dressing

A homage to the past, when iceberg was at the heart of all salads. An iceberg tip: Slam the bottom of the head on a wooden board and the core will simply fall out.

250 g/8 oz blue cheese

1 large head iceberg lettuce

8 slices bacon, cooked crisp and kept warm

Break the blue cheese into chunks and place it in a food processor. Process the cheese while adding 7 tablespoons cold water, a little at a time. Blend until completely smooth. Add some freshly ground black pepper. Chill until ready to use. Makes 250 ml/8 fl oz. If you like your dressing chunky, add 30 g/1 oz more crumbled blue cheese.

Cut the lettuce into 6 wedges. Pour blue cheese dressing over the top. Crumble the bacon into large pieces and sprinkle it over the tops of the lettuce wedges. Serve on chilled plates and pass the pepper mill.

Serves 6

Add a small clove of garlic, pushed through a garlic press, to the blue cheese dressing.

Swedish Cured Salmon

ADD-ONS

Delicious served with
hot Creamed
Potatoes Swedish-
Style (page 201). You
can also grill 185-g/
6-oz portions and
serve them medium-
rare.

GRAPENOTES

Serve with small
glasses of ice-cold
aquavit or vodka.

On any Swedish smorgasbord, once known as "the vodka table," you invariably find two or three preparations of gravlax—a curing, not a smoking, of whole sides of succulent salmon. Do as the Swedes do: Serve hot creamed potatoes as an accompaniment. Drink schnapps (chilled vodka or flavoured aquavit), with beer on the side.

1.5 kg/3 lb side of salmon, preferably the centre cut

60 g/2 oz sugar

90 g/3 oz freshly chopped dill, stalks included

Remove all the small bones from the salmon with tweezers. Pat the fish dry. Rub the salmon flesh with 45 g/1½ oz salt, 1 tablespoon coarse ground black pepper, the sugar, and the chopped dill. Cover with cling film. Weight down with a brick or other heavy object and refrigerate 48 to 72 hours.

Before serving, scrape off the dill and seasonings. Slice on an angle as if it were smoked salmon.

Serves 8 to 10

Sweet Mustard Sauce

It's funny how deprivation sometimes leads to discovery. With only three ingredients to play with, I left out the oil and egg generally used in making traditional Swedish mustard sauce for gravlax, prawns, and herring. And guess what?

3 tablespoons sugar
2 tablespoons distilled white vinegar
4 tablespoons Dijon mustard

Put the sugar and vinegar in a small bowl and stir until the sugar dissolves. Whisk in the mustard thoroughly with a wire whisk. Sauce will thicken.

Makes 125 ml/4 fl oz

ADD-ONS

Add 1 tablespoon finely chopped fresh dill.

Bresaola and Asiago "Carpaccio," Truffle Oil

ADD-ONS

You can roll the bresaola around a filling of rocket to make a roulade. Add shards of cheese and drizzle with truffle oil.

GRAPENOTE

Go Italian all the way, from a fruity Dolcetto to a more woodsy Spanna or Gattinara.

Heady flavours come together for an ultra-chic first course. Bresaola, air-dried beef from northern Italy, has an intense, gamey taste, while Asiago, cow's-milk cheese from the Veneto, has a rich, nutty flavour ending with a sharp note. With just a few drops of sensuous truffle oil, Carpaccio (a sixteenth-century Venetian painter) would surely have a satisfied palate! If you can't find bresaola, substitute Bündnerfleisch, which is air-dried cured beef from Austria or Switzerland.

250 g/8 oz thinly sliced bresaola

90 g/3 oz young Asiago cheese

1 tablespoon truffle oil

Cover 6 large plates with thinly sliced bresaola. Wrap tightly with cling film until ready to use.

Using a mandoline, a very sharp knife, or a cheese slicer, cut paper-thin slices of cheese. Scatter the cheese in the centre of the bresaola. Drizzle with truffle oil and sprinkle with coarse salt and coarse ground black pepper.

Serves 6

Celery Rémoulade, Celeriac Crisps

Celery rémoulade is part of every Paris bistro's hors d'oeuvre variés. France's mustardy answer to coleslaw, it is made with a variety of celery grown for its turnip-like root. My version adds unexpected crisps of roast celeriac.

750 g/1½ lb celery root (celeriac)

125 ml/4 fl oz plus 2 tablespoons light
    mayonnaise

3 tablespoons Dijon mustard

Preheat the oven to 200°C/400°F/gas 6.

Wash the celery root and peel. Cut two-thirds of the celery root into very thin julienne strips, about 5 cm/2 inches long.

Mix the mayonnaise and mustard together in a bowl and add the julienned celery root. Add salt and pepper to taste. Mix well and refrigerate.

Slice the remaining third of the celery root paper-thin. Place the slices on a baking tray, reduce the heat to 135°C/275°F/gas 1, and bake, turning once or twice, for 30 minutes, or until crisp. The celery root crisps will brown lightly, but do not let them get too dark.

Sprinkle with salt. Serve a mound of celery rémoulade with celeriac crisps on top.

Serves 5 to 6

ADD-ONS

Serve the salad on a bed of thinly sliced prosciutto or "speck," which is smoked prosciutto.

Roast Red Peppers,
Yellow Pepper Purée

ADD-ONS

Serve with a cruet of vinegar: red wine, balsamic, or Herbes de Provence (page 69).

GRAPENOTE

A mouth-filling, fruity chardonnay would do nicely.

If forced to pick my favourite vegetable, I'd choose a roast pepper. Sweet and meaty, it adds sex appeal to many dishes. But here it takes centre stage, a red one against a backdrop of yellow pepper purée.

6 large red peppers

4 large yellow peppers

125 ml/4 fl oz extra-virgin olive oil or Garlic Oil (page 52)

Hold the whole peppers over an open flame or place in the grill, turning periodically, until skins get very black on all sides. This will take 10 to 15 minutes in the grill.

Put the peppers in a brown paper bag and seal the bag to steam them. Let the peppers get cool enough to handle and peel the skins from the peppers. Core all the peppers but keep the red peppers whole, taking out the seeds from the centre. Put aside.

Cut the yellow peppers into strips, removing all the seeds. Purée the strips in a blender with the oil until creamy and emulsified. Add coarse salt and freshly ground black pepper.

To serve, spoon yellow pepper purée on the plates and top with the red peppers. Sprinkle with sea salt.

Serves 6

Herbes de Provence Vinegar

    500 ml/16 fl oz red wine vinegar
    2 teaspoons dried herbes de provence (see Note)
    1 long sprig of fresh rosemary

Combine all the ingredients in a small enamel saucepan with ½ teaspoon whole black peppercorns. Bring to a boil, turn off the heat, and let cool. Put in a jar with the herbs and cover tightly. Store in a cool, dark place.

Makes 500 ml/16 fl oz

Note: Available in speciality-food or spice shops.

Veal Sausage with Asparagus Sauce and Asparagus Tips

Grapenote

A white wine and a red wine will take this dish in two very different directions: A good warm-weather choice would be New Zealand's prized Cloudy Bay sauvignon blanc or the less pricey Stoneleigh; for cooler days try an elegant Sancerre Rouge from the Loire.

No one will believe that this dish, striking to look at and to taste, has only three ingredients. Use best-quality weisswurst from your delicatessen, although at a pinch supermarket bratwurst (a combination of veal and pork) will suffice.

> **500 g/1 lb fresh thin asparagus**
>
> **375 ml/12 fl oz homemade chicken broth (page 96) or canned**
>
> **4 to 5 fat veal sausages, weisswurst or bratwurst (750 g/1½ lb)**

Cut the tips off the asparagus stalks and reserve the tips for later use. Snap off the woody bottoms of the asparagus stalks and discard. Cut the remainder of each stalk into thirds.

Put the asparagus pieces and chicken broth in an enamel saucepan and cook over medium heat for 15 minutes, or until tender. Transfer the asparagus and broth to a blender. Purée 2 or 3 minutes, until sauce is very smooth. Makes 500 ml/16 fl oz.

Steam the sausages over boiling water for 8 to 10 minutes, or boil them for 5 minutes. Keep them warm.

Gently heat the asparagus sauce.

Blanch the asparagus tips in boiling water for 2 to 3 minutes. Drain.

Slice the sausages 12 mm/½ inch thick on the bias, place on a pool of sauce, and scatter with the asparagus tips.

Serves 4 or 5

Pan-Roasted Oysters with Butter and Leeks

"Palatable indulgence," said the great food writer Lucullus about the oyster. What would he have said about this dish? I say, Perfection, with a nice buttery chardonnay.

125 g/4 oz unsalted butter

2 pints fresh oysters, shucked, juice reserved

1 bunch leeks

Preheat the oven to 200°C/400°F/gas 6.

Use some of the butter to grease a shallow baking dish. Place the oysters in the dish. Melt the remaining butter in large nonstick frying pan. Reserve.

Trim the leeks, saving the white part only. Cut in half lengthwise, wash well, and pat dry. Julienne the leeks and add to the melted butter. Cook slowly for 15 minutes; then add 60 ml/2 fl oz of the reserved oyster juice, salt to taste, and 2 teaspoons whole black peppercorns.

Pour the leek mixture over the oysters and bake about 10 minutes, or until the edges begin to curl. Serve immediately.

Serves 4 to 6

ADD-ONS

Serve with Tiny Pepper Cheese Crackers (page 40). Add 125 ml/4 fl oz double cream to the pan juices and then a few tablespoons of dry vermouth. Serve in soup plates.

GRAPENOTE

A great match with a Puligny Montrachet, or the less expensive Rully.

Checkerboard Orzo Salad

ADD-ONS

Toss the tomato-cheese mixture with ½ tablespoon fresh thyme leaves.

Meticulously cut cubes of red tomatoes and firm white ricotta salata in this recipe remind me of a checkerboard—or of those charming check tablecloths found in trattorias. Equally homey is this refreshing conjunction of flavours and textures.

500 g/1 lb medium-size ripe tomatoes

185 g/6 oz ricotta salata, in one piece

250 g/8 oz uncooked orzo pasta

Carefully cut the tomatoes into neat little 10-mm/⅓-inch cubes and put the cubes in a shallow bowl. Cut the ricotta salata into the same size cubes. Add to tomatoes with a sprinkling of coarse salt and freshly ground black pepper. Let sit for 1 hour.

Bring a medium-size pan of salted water to a boil. Add the orzo and cook until tender, about 10 minutes. Drain. Put the orzo in a medium-size bowl and add half of the tomato-cheese mixture, along with any juices that have collected in the bottom of the bowl. Toss gently, adding salt to taste.

Put the orzo mixture on a platter and top with the remaining tomato-cheese mixture. Serve warm or at room temperature.

Serves 4

Niçoise Socca Crêpe, Marinated Goat Cheese

Socca, a kind of pizza made from chickpea flour, is an omnipresent snack in Nice. Here it's gone upscale with trendy goat cheese marinated in fruity, green olive oil. Use a British goat cheese or French Montrachet. Speaking of Montrachet, a glass of this chilled white Burgundy is an impressive partner.

> 8 thick slices of goat cheese, cut 2.5 cm/1 inch thick
>
> 80 ml/3 fl oz plus 80 ml/3 fl oz extra-virgin olive oil or Garlic Oil (page 52)
>
> 155 g/5 oz chickpea flour

Put the cheese in large shallow bowl or plate. Pour the 80 ml/3 fl oz oil over the top and sprinkle lightly with coarse salt. Let marinate 1 hour.

Sift the chickpea flour into a mixing bowl. Make a well and whisk in 125 ml/4 fl oz water to form a smooth, thick paste. Add another 125 ml/4 fl oz water, 2 tablespoons olive or garlic oil, ¼ teaspoon coarse salt, and a grinding of black pepper. Stir until very smooth.

Heat a 20-cm/8-inch nonstick frying pan until hot. Coat the bottom with 1 teaspoon olive oil. When it starts smoking, pour in a 60-ml/2-fl oz ladle of batter to cover the bottom evenly.

When the batter has set, turn over, adding a little more oil, and cook other side until golden. Remove to warm plates. Turn out onto a warm plate and repeat with the remaining batter to make 8 crêpes.

To serve, top each crêpe with marinated cheese.

Serves 8

GRAPENOTE

A great Montrachet or a full-bodied California chardonnay are perfect mates. A chilled Chiroubles from Beaujolais or a lighter-style pinot noir from California will be easier on the wallet.

Asparagus and Prosciutto Bundles, Melted Fontina

A member of the lily family, asparagus comes in three varieties: white, green and violet. Wrapped in a blanket of pink prosciutto, these are edible bundles of joy. Swathe them in a sauce of Italian fontina for a strong, nutty taste.

500 g/1 lb medium-size asparagus

125 g/4 oz thinly sliced prosciutto

185 g/6 oz Italian fontina cheese

Snap off the woody ends of the asparagus. Lightly scrape the stalks of the asparagus with a vegetable peeler.

Bring a pan of salted water to a boil. Add the asparagus and cook 8 to 10 minutes, until tender. With tongs, transfer the asparagus to a bowl of iced water to retain the bright green colour. Let sit for 5 minutes. Remove the asparagus and pat dry with kitchen paper.

Make 4 to 6 bundles of 5 to 6 asparagus each. Wrap each bundle with 2 slices of prosciutto, making a large pink band.

Cut the cheese into 2.5-cm/1-inch pieces. In a small, heavy saucepan, heat 2 tablespoons water. Add the cheese and stir with a wooden spoon until completely melted. When ready to serve, place bundles under the grill for 1 minute to warm. Quickly spoon cheese over asparagus bundles.

Serves 4 to 6

Wild Greens and Blood Orange Salad, Orange Vinaigrette

In the late 1980s, fancy wild greens became de rigueur in the best restaurants. Luckily for us, an inventive mix of lettuces that includes frisée, radicchio, red oakleaf, lamb's lettuce and, occasionally, edible flowers, is now available in some food stores. Substitute flavourful Valencia oranges if blood oranges are not in season.

185 g/6 oz wild greens (variety of mixed greens)

4 large blood oranges

60 ml/2 fl oz extra-virgin olive oil—plus additional for drizzling, if desired

Wash the lettuce and dry it completely. Reserve.

Grate the zest of 1 orange to make ½ teaspoon. Squeeze 1 to 2 oranges so you have 60 ml/2 fl oz juice.

In a small bowl, whisk together the orange juice, orange zest, and olive oil and season with ¼ teaspoon coarse salt and some freshly ground black pepper.

Remove the rind from the remaining oranges with a small, sharp knife. Cut in between the membranes to separate the orange segments and remove all membrane.

Pile the lettuce high on large chilled plates. Tuck the orange segments in and around the lettuce and spoon the dressing over the salad. If desired, drizzle additional olive oil around the edge of the salad.

Serves 4 or 5

Grilled Shiitake Mushrooms, Garlic Essence

ADD-ONS

Serve warm as a first course over White Polenta with Parmigiano-Reggiano (page 189), or cold as a salad with Roast Red Peppers, Yellow Pepper Purée (page 68). Scatter sprigs of fresh thyme or rosemary over the mushrooms while baking.

GRAPENOTES

"Big" and "bold" are the operative words: try a smoky fumé blanc reserve from Mondavi, or full-bodied chardonnay from Rosemount Estate, in Australia. Look for the words "barrel-fermented," "barrel-aged," or "reserve" on the label.

Unbeknownst to many of us, mushrooms are not vegetables but fungi that often taste like beef (the Japanese call this taste component umami). *Shiitake mushrooms are particularly meaty, with their dark-brown caps and bosky flavour. With a loaf of bread, this is almost a meal in itself.*

> 500 g/1 lb large shiitake mushrooms, wiped clean, stalks removed
>
> 3 tablespoons Garlic Oil (page 52), plus additional for drizzling
>
> 80 ml/3 fl oz dry white wine

Preheat the oven to 165°C/325°F/gas 3.

Line a baking tray with a piece of foil large enough to hold the mushrooms in a single layer. Sprinkle the foil with the garlic oil and wine. Place the mushrooms stalk side up on the baking tray and sprinkle with coarse salt and freshly ground pepper. Bake 20 minutes. Turn the mushrooms over and bake 10 minutes longer. Remove from the oven.

Slice the mushrooms thickly and serve with pan juices. Drizzle with additional garlic oil.

Serves 5 or 6

Seared Scallops
on Sweet Pea Purée

This lovely combination of sweet-fleshed scallops and sweet green peas is a perfect way to bring springtime into a meal in any season. Frozen petits pois, always available, produce the best results.

500 g/1 lb medium scallops (about 20)

1 (315-g/10-oz) package frozen petits pois, defrosted

50 g/1¾ oz unsalted butter

Pat the scallops dry with kitchen paper and reserve.

Put the peas in a small pan with just enough water to cover. Add ½ teaspoon coarse salt. Cook briefly over medium-high heat until the peas are tender but still bright green, about 2 minutes.

Drain the peas, saving 6 tablespoons cooking water and reserving 4 tablespoons peas for garnish. Put the peas in a blender and purée at highest speed. Add 30 g/1 oz of the butter, cut into small pieces, and 5 to 6 tablespoons cooking water, so that you have a very smooth but thick purée. You will have about 300 ml/10 fl oz purée. Keep warm.

In a large nonstick frying pan, melt 7 g/¼ oz of the remaining butter. Add the scallops and cook over high heat on both sides until golden.

In the centre of large plates, spread 80 ml/3 fl oz pea purée into a 13-cm/5-inch-diameter circle. Place the reserved peas, like pearls, around each circle. Remove the scallops from the pan with a slotted spoon. Arrange 5 scallops per dish on top of the pea purée.

Add 2 tablespoons dry vermouth to scallop pan juices.

GRAPENOTES

An oh-so-elegant marriage with a bottle of chilled Meursault or a more unusual riesling Kabinett from a good German producer.

Add 4 tablespoons reserved water to pan juices. Whisk in the remaining butter and remove from the heat; the sauce will thicken. Add salt to taste and pour the juices around the pea purée. Serve immediately.

Serves 4

Smoked Salmon "Pitza"

Shop-bought pita becomes an edible bed for flavoured cream cheese and warm smoked salmon. Great for brunch—or for dinner in your silk pyjamas. Just open a bottle of pink champagne! This dish is particularly memorable when made with "pastrami-cured salmon," a product occasionally available in speciality-food shops.

> 4 pita breads
>
> 125 g/4 oz herbed goat cheese or cream cheese
>
> 375 g/12 oz thinly sliced smoked salmon or pastrami-cured salmon (see Note)

Preheat the oven to 220°C/425°F/gas 7.

Lay the pita breads flat on a large baking tray. Whip the goat cheese until light and fluffy and spread the cheese evenly on the pita breads, leaving a border of 12 mm/½ inch. Place the smoked salmon evenly on top to completely cover the cheese.

Bake 6 or 7 minutes, until salmon is warmed.

Serve on individual plates. If desired, cut each into 6 wedges, using a pizza cutter or very sharp knife.

Serves 4

Note: Pastrami-cured salmon is cured and smoked with spices typically used for pastrami: coriander seed, bay leaves, garlic.

ADD-ONS

Sprinkle with tiny nonpareil capers and finely diced red onion.

GRAPENOTES

Try a bottle of a pink champagne.

Tomato, Mozzarella and Basil: Six Styles

"In cooking, as in all arts, simplicity is the sign of perfection."

CURNONSKY

**1 to 1.5 kg/2 to 3 lb very large ripe tomatoes
(6), depending on recipe**

**500 to 750 g/1 to 1½ lb freshly made
mozzarella cheese, depending on recipe**

1 large bunch fresh basil

TOMATO PURÉE

Peel 1 or 2 ripe tomatoes, cut in half and squeeze out seeds. Put in a blender and frappé with a pinch of sea salt until smooth and frothy.

BASIL PURÉE

Place 15 g/½ oz washed, dried, and tightly packed basil leaves in a blender. Add 2 to 3 tablespoons cold water and purée until very smooth. Add sea salt to taste and blend until incorporated.

I. Mozzarella with Julienned Tomato and Basil

Cut *500 g/1 lb fresh mozzarella* into 6 thick slices, and spread them on a plate in a single layer or slightly overlapping. Cut the outer flesh off *3 large tomatoes*, reserving pulp, and cut into thin strips. Put in a bowl. Julienne as many fresh basil leaves as needed to equal the volume of the tomato strips. Add to the bowl and toss together with a pinch of sea salt. Place a mound of the julienned mixture on top of the cheese. Drizzle with 1½ tablespoons basil purée. Finely chop the reserved tomato pulp and use as a garnish surrounding the cheese.

II. Tomato, Basil, and Mozzarella Flower

Cut a large, thick slice of tomato from the centre of *6 tomatoes* with stems. Put the slices in a blender and purée with a pinch of sea salt. Cut *500 g/1 lb fresh mozzarella* into 6 thick slices. Using the remaining tomato parts, make "sandwiches" with mozzarella and fresh basil leaves as filling. Sprinkle with sea salt and freshly ground black pepper. Place on a pool of tomato purée.

III. Baked Tomato, Mozzarella, and Basil

Preheat the oven to 200°C/400°F/gas 6. Cut 12 mm/½ inch off the tops of *4 tomatoes* and reserve. Scoop out the tomato pulp and reserve. Place 2 large basil leaves in the bottom of each tomato shell. Cut *250 g/½ lb fresh mozzarella* into 4 pieces. Fill each shell with cheese. Bake 8 to 10 minutes, until the cheese melts. Garnish with fresh basil leaves. Optional: Serve warm with tomato or basil purée.

IV. Mozzarella and Tomato Skewers

Place *4 tomatoes* stem side down. Make 4 slits almost to the bottom of each tomato, about 12mm/½ inch apart. Cut *750 g/1½ pounds fresh mozzarella* into 16 slices. Slip a piece of cheese into each slit, trimming excess cheese away with small sharp knife. Place two long wooden or decorative metal skewers lengthwise into each tomato. Cut between skewers. You will have 8 skewers. Sprinkle with sea salt and coarse ground black pepper. Serve on a bed of fresh basil leaves.

V. Tomato and Mozzarella Pinwheels

Cut *3 tomatoes* into 9 thick slices (discard the tops and bottoms). Cut the slices in half to produce 18 half circles. Cut *625 g/1¼ pounds fresh mozzarella* into 9 slices and cut into half circles. Alternate cheese and tomatoes on plates in pinwheel fashion. Place basil leaves in centre. Decorate the edges of the plates with teaspoonfuls of basil purée.

VI. Tomato and Mozzarella "Club"

Cut 12 mm/½ inch off the tops and bottoms of *6 tomatoes* and discard. Cut the tomatoes in half horizontally. Cut *500 g/1 lb fresh mozzarella* into 6 thick slices. Sandwich cheese and fresh basil leaves between thick tomato slices, trimming off excess cheese to make the cheese conform to the tomatoes' shapes. Place 4 cocktail sticks in each "sandwich," cut in quarters vertically, and turn quarters with points facing out. Serve with tomato purée, if desired.

I, II, V, and VI: Serves 6
III and IV: Serves 4

Salad Frisée with Lardons and Hot Vinegar Dressing

In abundantly stocked vegetable markets, you often find wispy heads of jade-green frisée from France. Heartier home-grown frisée makes a more assertive substitute. This is a warming first course that can easily become a main course with the addition of wholewheat croutons and Roquefort cheese.

2 large heads frisée lettuce

250 g/8 oz pancetta, in 6-mm/¼-inch slices

125 ml/4 fl oz good-quality red wine vinegar, or Herbes de Provence Vinegar (page 69)

Wash the lettuce and dry well in a salad spinner. Tear the leaves coarsely. Reserve.

Cut pancetta slices into 6-mm/¼-inch-wide strips, or lardons. Cook over medium heat in a nonstick frying pan until the fat is rendered and the pancetta is beginning to crisp. Remove the pancetta with a slotted spoon; reserve the rendered fat in the frying pan.

Divide the lettuce evenly onto 4 to 6 plates. Divide the pancetta evenly over the lettuce.

Add the vinegar carefully to the hot fat in the pan. Cook over high heat for 1 minute, adding a pinch of salt. Pour the hot dressing over the lettuce. Serve immediately and add pepper to taste.

Serves 4 to 6

Delicious with crumbled blue cheese on top of the salad.

Chapter 8

Soups and Pasta

Soups and pasta, often designated for the beginning of a meal, are also meals in themselves. Sometimes soup and pasta even coexist in a single dish, as in Fennel, Leek and Orzo Soup, or Ginger Pepperpot, "Glass" Noodles.

In the Italian culture, pasta is an individual course—a bridge between the antipasto and the main course. Rarely does it take centre stage. But here, where the structure of one's repast is as individual as one's mode of dress, pasta is "as you like it!"

Carrot-Ginger Velvet

GRAPENOTE

An off-dry gewürz-
traminer would be a
lovely choice.

The development of a recipe: Sounded delicious in my head, could almost taste it, could see its brilliant colour and feel its creamy texture— like velvet on my tongue. But it took many tries to get it right.

> 750 g/1½ lb fresh carrots (with carrot tops, if possible), plus 2 large carrots for roasting (see Note)
>
> 7.5-cm/3-inch piece of fresh ginger, yielding 1½ teaspoons ginger juice (see Note)
>
> 125 ml/4 fl oz double cream

Trim the carrots, saving the tops. Peel the carrots and cut them into 2.5-cm/1-inch pieces. Put them in a medium-size pan with 1 litre/ 32 fl oz water and 1½ teaspoons salt. Bring to a boil, lower the heat, and cook, covered, for 35 minutes, or until the carrots are very soft.

Transfer the carrots to a food processor and purée until very smooth, slowly adding cooking water as you go. All the water should be incorporated. Add the ginger juice and double cream and process.

Gently heat the soup before serving, adding a few tablespoons of water if necessary.

Serve with julienned roast carrots and a few leaves from the carrot tops.

Makes 1 litre/32 fl oz , serving 4 or 5

Notes: To roast carrots: Preheat the oven to 200°C/400°F/gas 6. Put the washed, unpeeled carrots in a roasting tin and bake 50 minutes, or until soft. Let cool. Peel. Cut into match-stick-size julienne.

To prepare ginger juice: Peel the ginger with a small, sharp knife. Grate on the large holes of a hand grater. Put the grated ginger in kitchen paper and squeeze the juice from ginger. You will have about 1½ to 2 teaspoons.

Port Consommé

You expect consommé to start a meal, but this fine soup also is a sophisticated "intermezzo" to cleanse the palate between courses. It is so interesting in flavour, it could even "consummate" a meal, after the cheese course but before the cigars.

180 ml/6 fl oz tawny port wine

1 cinnamon stick

750 ml/24 fl oz beef broth

Put the port, the cinnamon stick, and ¼ teaspoon whole black peppercorns in a small, heavy enamel pan. Reduce over low heat to 125 ml/4 fl oz

Meanwhile, in another pan, reduce the beef broth slowly until it becomes 600 ml/1 pint.

Pour the reduced port through a sieve and add it to the reduced beef broth. Heat gently before serving.

Serves 6

"Cream" of Spinach Soup

Add-Ons

Shave Parmigiano-
Reggiano on top, or
dust lightly with
freshly grated nutmeg.

In the Italian kitchen, the word crema *when used for soups refers to a smooth, thick texture, not necessarily to the addition of cream. There's no cream here either, but lots of fresh spinach and potatoes bound with butter. This is comfort food at its most brilliant—in colour, that is.*

500 g/1 lb boiling potatoes, peeled

500 g/1 lb fresh spinach leaves, stems removed

75 g/2½ oz unsalted butter

In a large, heavy pan, bring 2 litres/64 fl oz of water to a boil with 1 teaspoon salt. Halve the potatoes lengthwise and cut halves into 12-mm/½-inch-thick slices. Put the slices in the pan and cook over medium-high heat for 20 minutes.

Add the spinach and cook 10 minutes longer. Do not overcook, or the spinach will lose its bright-green colour.

Transfer the spinach and potatoes to a food processor with a slotted spoon, reserving 600 ml/1 pint cooking liquid. Process until very smooth, adding the butter a little at a time.

Put the spinach purée back in the pan and slowly add the cooking liquid until you reach the desired consistency. Reheat gently and add salt and pepper to taste. Serve hot.

Makes 2 litres/64 fl oz, serving 8 to 10

Fournade: Creamy Chickpea Soup

This unusual soup is a speciality of southern France (and Liguria, where it is known as panizza), *but a touch of aromatic Egyptian spices, called dukkah, makes it quite global. Add a few drops of truffle oil and this humble "soupe au bâton" (literally "stirred with a stick") is deserving of a silver spoon.*

155 g/5 oz chickpea flour

1 litre/32 fl oz chicken or vegetable broth, preferably homemade

4 tablespoons extra-virgin olive oil

Combine the chickpea flour and broth in the bowl of an electric mixer and beat until smooth. Pour into a large heavy pan and add 2 tablespoons of the olive oil, 1 teaspoon salt and ⅛ teaspoon each finely ground white and black pepper.

Bring to a boil, then immediately lower the heat and simmer 10 minutes, stirring often with a wooden spoon or wire whisk. The soup will thicken quickly. Add water to thin as desired. Drizzle with the remaining 2 tablespoons of oil.

Makes about 1 litre/32 fl oz, serving 6

Add-Ons

Sprinkle with some Egyptian spices, or a few drops of truffle oil.

Egyptian spices:
2 tablespoons sesame seeds

1 tablespoon coriander seeds

2 teaspoons cumin seeds

Put the spices in a nonstick frying pan and cook a few minutes over low heat until fragrant. Grind to a fine powder in a spice grinder. Put in a small bowl and add a liberal pinch of salt.

Soupy Red Beans with Smoked Ham

Make enough to last a week, because the simple flavours deepen day by day. A flourish of sweet-and-sour greens will make your mouth water. Follow with Spoonbread Custard (page 188).

500 g/1 lb dried red kidney beans

2 medium onions, peeled and quartered

**1 smoked ham hock, split, or 250 g/8 oz
    smoked streaky bacon**

Pick over the beans and wash them. Soak them overnight in cold water to cover by 5 cm/2 inches.

Drain the beans. Put them in a pan with fresh water to cover by 5 cm/2 inches. Add the onions and ham hock. Bring to a boil, lower the heat, and cover, and simmer the beans 1 hour, periodically skimming off the foam that rises to the surface. Add 2 teaspoons salt and cook 1½ hours longer over low heat, uncovered. Stir often. The beans will be very tender and the soup will thicken.

Add freshly ground black pepper to taste. Cut off any meat from the bones, dice it, and add it to the beans. Serve hot.

Makes about 1 litre/32 fl oz, serving 6 to 8

ADD-ONS

Serve with Pickled Greens (page 91). Add a few bay leaves and 2 peeled cloves of garlic to the pan when cooking. To make this soup a main course, serve over fluffy long-grain rice.

GRAPENOTE

Served with a glass of spicy cold gewürztraminer, this is an interesting way to begin a dinner. As a meal in itself, try it with a good Belgian beer.

Pickled Greens

An unusual preparation of bitter greens that winds up sweet and sassy. Use as a cool topping for Soupy Red Beans (page 90), or alongside some Barbecued Pork Pull (page 158).

> 500 g/1 lb bitter greens or kale
> 185 g/6 oz sugar
> 125 ml/4 fl oz vinegar

Wash, dry, and coarsely chop the greens, including stems. In a large pan, combine 500 ml/16 fl oz water, the sugar, the vinegar, 1½ tablespoons salt and 1 teaspoon whole black peppercorns. Bring to a boil, lower the heat, and cook 5 minutes.

Add the greens to the pan. Cook 2 minutes. Let cool. Pack in a 1-litre/ 32- fl oz jar with lid. Cover and let sit 2 days, refrigerated, before using.

Makes 1 litre/32 fl oz

Avocado Velouté, Fino Sherry

This is a chilled soup with a haunting aftertaste. It is three-ingredient alchemy, because this dish tastes nothing like its components. No one will guess what it is, but everyone will ask for more.

> 1 large ripe avocado
>
> 375 ml/12 fl oz homemade chicken broth
>   (page 96) or canned
>
> 1 tablespoon fino sherry

Remove the stone from the avocado and then peel the avocado with a sharp knife. Cut into 12-mm/½-inch pieces. Put the chicken broth and 250 ml/8 fl oz water in a medium-size heavy saucepan and bring to a boil. Lower the heat and add the avocado. Simmer 2 minutes.

Transfer the contents of the saucepan to a blender. Process until the soup is very smooth and creamy. Stir in the sherry and chill well.

Makes 875 ml/28 fl oz

ADD-ONS

Garnish with a dollop of crème fraîche or chopped smoked almonds.

GRAPENOTE

Serve with small glass of fino sherry.

Fennel, Leek and Orzo Soup

The most Italian of vegetables, fennel has marvellous digestive proper-ties—which is a good thing, because this soup thickens like porridge. It is an Italian custom to put the sweet and versatile finocchio *on the table, like a fruit, at the end of a meal.*

1 large bulb fennel, finely diced, about 750 g/1½ pounds

3 large leeks

185 g/6 oz uncooked orzo

Cut off the fennel fronds from the fennel bulb and reserve for a garnish. Remove any brown spots from the fennel bulb.

Clean the leeks thoroughly and dice finely.

Put 2 litres/64 fl oz water in a large, heavy pan and bring to a boil. Add the fennel and orzo and 1½ teaspoons salt. Lower the heat, cover, and simmer 50 minutes.

With a large ladle, remove 1 litre/32 fl oz of soup from the pan and purée until smooth in a food processor. Return the soup to the pan and continue to cook, uncovered, over medium heat for 8 to 10 min-utes. Add salt and freshly ground black pepper to taste. Chop the fennel fronds and use them to garnish the soup.

Makes 2.75 litres/4½ pints, serving 10

Drizzle with extra-virgin olive oil or freshly grated Parmesan cheese. The next day, when the soup is very thick, serve with a poached egg on top.

Curried Lentil Soup

ADD-ONS

Add a splash of
Madeira to the hot
soup before serving.

*This could be my soupe du jour 365 days a year. A soupçon of
Madeira makes a big splash by transforming this legume into something
lusty and aromatic. But it's great even without it.*

125 g/4 oz French green lentils

90 g/3 oz finely chopped shallots

2 teaspoons good-quality curry powder

Put the lentils, the shallots, the curry powder, 1 litre/32 fl oz of water
and 2 teaspoons salt in a medium-size heavy saucepan and bring to a
boil. Lower heat, cover, and simmer 25 minutes, or until tender.

Process in a food processor until smooth. The soup will still have a
rough texture because of the lentils. You could pass it through a sieve,
but I find the roughness appealing.

Makes 500 ml/16 fl oz, serving 2

Note: French green lentils are found at speciality-food stores.

"Fire and Ice" Gazpacho

Add as much fire as you desire. Flash-chill in the freezer just until ice crystals begin to appear, then serve. Add a splash of pepper vodka just for fun.

500 ml/16 fl oz passata or strained tomatoes

1½ tablespoons hot sauce (see Note)

2 large red peppers (375 g/¾ lb)

Put the tomatoes and hot sauce in a medium-size bowl.

Core and seed the peppers and process in a food processor until puréed.

Add the pepper purée to the tomatoes. Mix well and transfer to a medium-size heavy enamel pan. Simmer 10 minutes and add freshly ground black pepper to taste.

Let cool, then chill in the refrigerator until very cold.

Serves 3 or 4

ADD-ONS

Add chopped cooked prawns, diced avocado, soured cream, coriander leaves, or chopped cucumber as a garnish.

GRAPENOTE

Serve a short glass of iced pepper vodka on the side. Or keep the "fire" low and go for a fino. If you add lots of "fire" to the dish, go with a very "hoppy" beer.

Note: Do not Tabasco, it is much too concentrated.

Chicken Broth 1-2-3

I'm a morning kind of person and love to start cooking early in the day, especially on the weekends, when I generally make soups and stocks. Even if you've never made stock before, here's a satisfying way to start.

This stock is easy, but give it time to simmer gently. "The pot should only smile with heat" (French proverb). Once the soup is strained, you can reduce it further until it becomes thick and syrupy, for what professionals call glace de volaille.

> **2.5 kg/5 lb chicken pieces**
>
> **375 g/12 oz carrots, with carrot tops**
>
> **4 large onions**

Wash the chicken pieces and pat dry with kitchen paper. Peel the carrots and cut them into 2.5-cm/1-inch pieces. Wash the carrot tops and chop enough for 125 ml/4 fl oz. Peel the onions and cut into thin wedges.

Put all ingredients in a large heavy pan with 5 to 6 litres/8 to 10 pints cold water to cover and 1 teaspoon whole black peppercorns. Bring just to a boil, lower the heat, and simmer 2½ hours, skimming off any foam that forms on the surface.

Line a sieve with muslin and pour the broth through into a large bowl. At this point you can put the strained broth in a large clean pan and reduce to desired consistency.

Let the broth cool and refrigerate it until ready to use, removing any fat. If serving as soup, return the strained broth to the pan, add the cooked onions and carrots, heat, and serve. The broth or soup can be kept for up to two days. Before using broth, skim the fat, then bring to a boil and boil for 5 minutes to eliminate any bacteria. Makes about 4 litres/6 pints. If reducing to use as a stock, reduce to 3 litres/5 pints.

"Sopa de Salsa"

Totally fun. Serve in large colourful mugs with a basket of warm taco chips. Control the heat with your choice of salsa, from mild to incendiary. Serve with beer and you've got a great little meal.

ADD-ONS

Garnish with a dollop of soured cream or Crisp Tortilla Ribbons (page 98).

875 ml/28 fl oz single cream

1 medium onion, finely chopped

1 (375-g/12-oz) jar medium-hot salsa

Bring the cream and onions to a boil in a medium-size pan. Lower the heat and simmer for 15 minutes. Add the salsa, and simmer 5 minutes. Purée in a blender.

Pour the soup back into the pan and simmer 5 minutes or until hot, letting the flavours mingle.

Makes 1.2 litres/35 fl oz, serving 4 or 5

Crisp Tortilla Ribbons

2 corn tortillas
2 tablespoons vegetable oil

Cut the tortillas into 2-mm/$\frac{1}{16}$-inch-wide ribbons. In a small nonstick frying pan, heat the oil and fry the ribbons until crisp. Drain and sprinkle lightly with salt. Set aside until ready to use.

Makes 4 to 5 portions

Yellow Turnip Soubise

In the classic French repertoire, a soubise sauce is made from onions and thickened with rice. This soup incorporates onions and rice plus the pleasing, burnished flavour of slow-roasted swedes, also known as rutabagas or Swedish turnips.

> **1 kg/2 lb swedes, peeled and trimmed, cut into large chunks**
>
> **500 g/1 lb onions, peeled and cut into large chunks**
>
> **6 tablespoons long-grain rice**

Put the swedes, the onions, 1.5 litres/48 fl oz water, and 2 teaspoons salt in a large heavy pan and bring to a boil. Add the rice, mix well, and cover. Lower heat and simmer 50 minutes, or until vegetables are very soft.

In several batches, purée contents of pan in a food processor until very, very smooth. Return the purée to the pan. Adjust the seasoning with salt and freshly ground black pepper.

Reheat before serving. This soup gets better as it sits and is decidedly better the next day.

Makes 2.4 litres/4 pints, serving 9 to 10

ADD-ONS

Garnish with coarsely chopped fresh tarragon leaves. Pass a small jug of double cream for those who will.

GRAPENOTE

Its sweet, earthy essence makes this soup a good match with a California viognier, a white Côtes du Rhône, or a white Rioja.

Beer and Stilton Soup

Don't expect a bowl of something thick and creamy, because this unusual preparation is a heady consommé worthy of sophisticated guests. Use amber beer from a local microbrewery—and during the Christmas season try a sweeter beer. Very après-ski.

If you want a thicker soup, dissolve 1 tablespoon arrowroot in 1 tablespoon cold water. Whisk into the hot soup and cook until soup thickens. Garnish with fresh chervil. Serve with homemade Beer Bread (opposite) or caraway rye.

GRAPENOTES

A real "taste match" with Alsatian riesling from Trimbach, or an ice-cold beer of your choice.

> 1.5 litres/48 fl oz homemade chicken broth (page 96) or canned
>
> 375 ml/12 fl oz amber beer
>
> 375g/12 oz mature Stilton cheese

In a medium-size heavy pan, bring chicken broth and beer to a rapid boil. Lower the heat and cook over medium heat for 20 minutes, or until liquid is reduced to 1.25 litres/2 pints.

Crumble the Stilton into small pieces and add it to the simmering broth, slowly stirring with a wooden spoon. Add freshly ground pepper to taste. Continue to cook for 5 to 10 minutes, until slightly thickened.

Makes 1.4 litres/44 fl oz, serving 5 or 6

Beer Bread

6 tablespoons sugar
375 ml/12 fl oz beer, at room temperature
470 g/15 oz self-raising flour

Preheat the oven to 190°C/350°F/gas 5.

Place the sugar in a medium-size enamel pan and cook over medium heat until it is caramelized. Remove from the heat when the sugar is a light-brown liquid.

Pour in the beer slowly. The liquid will foam and bubble. Mix well with a wooden spoon until all the sugar is dissolved.

Put the flour in the bowl of an electric mixer. Add a pinch of salt and slowly pour in the liquid. Mix until the ingredients are incorporated and the dough is smooth.

Place the dough in a 23-cm/9-inch nonstick loaf tin. Bake 55 to 60 minutes; the bread is done when a cocktail stick comes out clean. Remove bread from the oven and let cool on a rack.

Makes one loaf

Red Wine Onion Soup

It has been said that the only good onion soup is a simple one. And it doesn't get more simple than this! Substitute beef broth for wine for a more classic rendition. Make sure the onions are thoroughly caramelized (dark brown and soft), for the deepest, sweetest flavour.

> 50 g/1¾ oz unsalted butter
>
> 1 kg/2 lb onions, peeled, halved, and thinly sliced
>
> 250 ml/8 fl oz cabernet sauvignon or other robust red wine

Melt the butter in large heavy pan with a cover. Add the onions and sauté over medium heat for 30 to 40 minutes, until onions are soft and caramelized (they will be a deep-brown colour). Stir often, scraping up the browned bits with a wooden spoon.

Add the wine and cook, stirring frequently, until most of the liquid has evaporated.

Add 1.5 litres/48 fl oz water, 2 teaspoons salt and freshly ground white pepper to taste. Bring to a boil. Lower the heat, cover and simmer 20 minutes. Purée 500 ml/16 fl oz of soup (with onions) in a food processor until smooth.

Add this mixture to the soup pan and cook 10 minutes longer, uncovered. Serve very hot.

Makes 1.6 litres/2½ pints, serving 4 to 6

ADD-ONS

Serve the soup with grated Asiago cheese, or put a toasted crouton on the top of each bowl of soup and cover with a thin slice of fontina or Gruyère cheese. Put under the grill until the cheese begins to melt and brown lightly.

GRAPENOTE

Often a fruity Beaujolais is a good companion to classic onion soup, but this soup should be served with the same full-bodied cabernet used in the dish.

An Unusual Borscht: Roast Beetroot, Squash and Yogurt

There are as many borschts as there are former members of the Soviet Union, but the unifying ingredient is generally the scarlet beetroot. This recipe gains its intense flavour from roasting the vegetables before puréeing them.

750 g/1½ lb large beetroot with green tops

1 kg/2 lb winter squash

250 ml/8 fl oz natural yogurt

Preheat the oven to 200°C/400°F/gas 6.

Wash the beetroot. Remove the green tops and reserve. Cut the beetroot in half. Cut the squash in quarters and remove the seeds. Place the beetroot and squash cut side down in a baking tin. Sprinkle with 60 ml/2 fl oz water. Roast for 1½ hours, or until soft. (Turn the vegetables over halfway through cooking, adding more water if necessary.)

Remove from the oven and let cool 10 minutes. Remove the squash pulp from the skin and purée it in a food processor. Peel the beetroot, cut them into small pieces, and add them to the processor. Purée until smooth. Add the yogurt and purée again. Add 80 to 125 ml/3 to 4 fl oz cold water and 1 teaspoon salt. Process until smooth and creamy. Serve hot or cold.

Garnish with additional yogurt, or with beetroot greens that have been steamed and chopped.

Makes about 1 litre/32 fl oz, serving 4 to 5

ADD-ONS

If not using beetroot greens, garnish with finely chopped onions or spring onions, or chopped cucumber. Serve with Caraway Cheese Crisps (see page 104).

Caraway Cheese Crisps

1 medium-size loaf unsliced rye bread with caraway seeds
90 g/3 oz unsalted butter
60 g/2 oz grated Parmesan cheese

Preheat the oven to 135°C/275°F/gas 1. With a sharp knife, slice the bread paper-thin. Melt the butter in the saucepan and add the cheese. Spread the mixture on one side of each slice of bread. Place the bread on an ungreased baking tray and bake for 20 to 25 minutes, until the edges start to curl and the bread is crisp. Stores well.

Makes 30 crisps

Chilled Cauliflower Crème

Here's an elegant way to serve this aggressive relative of the cabbage. But don't keep it more than a day or two, because its cabbagey essence will surely grow.

> **1 large head cauliflower**
>
> **1 bunch spring onions (5–6)**
>
> **125 ml/4 fl oz single cream**

Trim the cauliflower of its green leaves. Separate the cauliflower into florets and chop the core into pieces. In a large pan, put all the cauliflower, 875 ml/28 fl oz water, and 1¾ teaspoons salt.

Trim the spring onions. Remove the dark-green tops and save. Cut the remaining white and light-green parts into 2.5-cm/1-inch lengths and add them to the pan.

Bring to a boil. Lower the heat, cover, and cook 20 to 25 minutes, until very soft. Transfer the contents of the pan to the bowl of a food processor and purée until very smooth. You may need to do this in two batches. Add the cream and freshly ground white pepper. Refrigerate until very cold.

Garnish with spring onion tops that have been finely chopped.

Makes 1.4 litres/44 fl oz, serving 5 to 6

ADD-ONS

Delicious served in small chilled cups with a teaspoon of black caviar on top.

GRAPENOTE

If serving with caviar, celebrate with a fairly yeasty sparkler with some bottle age: Schramsberg blanc de noirs or Charles Heidsieck.

Brie and Pear Soup

ADD-ONS

Garnish with whole
pink peppercorns or
lightly toasted sliced
almonds.

GRAPENOTE

Nice with a glass
of bold, floral
chardonnay.

*According to Ralph Waldo Emerson, "there are only ten minutes in the
life of a pear when it is perfect to eat." Luckily, this soup is perfect any-
time. Use Bartlett pears in the early autumn, ripe Comice in the winter,
fragrant Bosc and Anjou when available. Make sure the Brie is also ripe
—preferably a* double-crème *from France.*

> **2 large ripe pears (about 500 g/1 lb)**
>
> **500 ml/16 fl oz homemade chicken broth
> (page 96) or canned**
>
> **250 g/8 oz double-cream Brie cheese**

Peel the pears. Cut them into thick slices, removing the seeds. Put
the chicken broth and pears in a large pan and simmer 10 to 15
minutes, until the pears are very soft.

Transfer the pears and broth to a food processor and process until
very smooth. Return to the pan and simmer.

Trim the rind from the brie and cut the cheese into small pieces.
Slowly add the cheese and stir with a wooden spoon until melted. The
soup should be creamy and smooth.

Serves 4 or 5

Ginger Pepperpot, "Glass" Noodles

Ginger juice is easily extracted: Grate a knobby chunk of peeled fresh ginger root on a hand grater; wrap the shavings in a kitchen paper and gently squeeze.

Cellophane noodles made from bean curd look like strings of glass. You can use soba noodles or angel hair pasta as a substitute.

1.5 litres/48 fl oz homemade chicken broth
(page 96) or canned

125-g/4-oz piece fresh ginger root

125 g/4 oz cellophane noodles

ADD-ONS
Garnish with finely chopped spring onions and/or fresh coriander leaves. The soup can also be served with strips of cooked chicken or roast pork.

In a large heavy pan, toast ½ teaspoon white peppercorns until fragrant. Add the chicken broth and bring to a boil. Lower the heat and simmer 20 minutes, or until the broth is reduced to 1.1 litres/36 fl oz.

Meanwhile, peel the ginger root. Cut off a 2.5-cm/1-inch piece and mince; you will have about 1 tablespoon. Set aside in a small bowl. Grate the rest of the ginger root on the large holes of hand grater. Put the grated ginger root in a piece of kitchen paper and squeeze the juice into another small bowl. You should have about 4½ teaspoons juice. Add to the minced ginger root.

When the broth has reduced, add the ginger juice, minced ginger root, and cellophane noodles. Cook 5 minutes, or until noodles are soft.

Serves 4

Sauerkraut "Hangover" Soup

This is the best way I know to cure a hangover and have a comforting meal at the same time (but then again, I'm of Hungarian descent). Serve with little sandwiches of buttered black bread.

> 500 g/1 lb packaged sauerkraut
>
> 3½ tablespoons dark soft brown sugar
>
> 1 (880-g/28-oz) can crushed tomatoes in juice

Put sauerkraut with its liquid and 3 tablespoons of the brown sugar in a large enamel pan and cook over medium heat for 5 minutes.

Add the crushed tomatoes and juice. Add 500 ml/16 fl oz water, 1 teaspoon salt, and freshly ground white and black pepper. Cover and simmer 30 minutes. Add remaining ½ tablespoon brown sugar, to balance flavours. Cook 1 to 2 minutes uncovered. Serve hot.

Makes 1.75 litres/56 fl oz, serving 7 to 8

ADD-ONS

Sprinkle the soup with caraway seeds. Or put the soup in onion-soup crocks, place a slice of mild Cheddar cheese on top, and grill for 30 seconds, or until cheese melts and begins to brown.

GRAPENOTE

If you don't have a hangover, try a good dark beer named Samuel . . . Adams or Smith.

Yellow Pea and Bacon Potage

The humourist Bennett Cerf described good manners as "the noise you don't make when you're eating soup." So put manners aside and enjoy. This is one of my favourites.

250 g/8 oz dried yellow split peas

60 g/2 oz medium-size onions

4 slices bacon, cut into 12-mm/½-inch pieces

Soak the yellow peas overnight.

The next day, peel the onions and cut them into 8 wedges.

Put the bacon in a medium-size heavy pan and cook 1 to 2 minutes, until the fat begins to melt. Add the onions and sauté the bacon and onions over medium heat for 10 minutes, or until they begin to brown lightly.

Add the drained yellow peas and 750 ml/24 fl oz of fresh water. Bring to a boil, lower the heat, and cook, covered, for 45 minutes, stirring often.

Purée 250 ml/8 fl oz of the soup in a blender and add it back to the soup pan with ½ teaspoon salt. Cook 5 or 6 minutes, adding more water if soup is too thick.

Makes 1.1 litres/36 fl oz, serving 4 or 5

ADD-ONS

Sprinkle with a little finely snipped fresh sage.

GRAPENOTE

This soup is a good candidate for an Alsatian pinot blanc; a good imported Pilsner would also be appropriate.

Veal Tortellini,
Turkish Yogurt Sauce

ADD-ONS

Add ½ teaspoon
sweet paprika to the
melted butter. This
dish also works with
tortellini filled with
spinach.

GRAPENOTE

Delicious paired with
your favourite flavour-
packed sauvignon
blanc.

Gail, my globe-trotting sister-in-law, lived in Istanbul for five years. In addition to being fluent in Turkish (and Japanese), she is a fabulous cook and often uses this simple Turkish sauce as a topping for pasta. She makes her own tortellini—but you can buy yours.

> **500 g/1 lb veal tortellini**
>
> **250 ml/8 fl oz Labaneh (opposite), at room temperature**
>
> **30 g/1 oz unsalted butter**

Boil the tortellini in salted water—they will rise to the top of the pan when done. While the pasta is cooking, beat the labaneh with a whisk until it loosens. Make sure it is at room temperature.

Drain the pasta well in a colander. Place it in a serving bowl and top with the labaneh. Quickly melt the butter, being careful not to let it brown, and pour it over the pasta. Pass the pepper mill.

Serves 4 to 5

Labaneh
(Yogurt Cheese)

500 ml/16 fl oz low fat natural yogurt
½ clove garlic (optional)

Line a sieve with two layers of muslin. Place the yogurt in the sieve. Place the sieve over a bowl to catch the liquid. Let sit at room temperature 8 hours, or until very thick.

If using garlic, push it through a garlic press and add it to the labaneh. Stir well and refrigerate.

Makes 250 ml/8 fl oz

Garlic and Oil Spaghetti

My best friend, Arthur Schwartz, food critic of New York's Daily News *and host of a popular radio show, says, "Fifty million Italians can't be wrong! Spaghetti 'aglio e olio' is like mother's milk in the land of macaroni."*

4 medium cloves garlic

6 tablespoons fruity olive oil

250 g/8 oz spaghetti

Bring a large pan of salted water to a boil.

Peel the garlic and finely chop. In a small frying pan, combine the garlic and olive oil and cook the garlic over low heat until it is pale brown. Do not let it get darker or it will be bitter.

Drain the spaghetti when done ("al dente" for many brands takes 12 minutes), saving 80 ml/3 fl oz of the cooking water.

Put the 80 ml/3 fl oz cooking water, the garlic, the oil, and the well-drained pasta in a large, heated serving bowl. Toss gently and season to taste with salt and pepper.

Serves 3 or 4

ADD-ONS

Add 1½ teaspoons hot red pepper flakes when browning the garlic.

GRAPENOTE

Arthur says to serve an unpretentious, simple red wine from Italy. And yes, you *can* still get Chianti in a straw basket, or *fiasco!*

Linguine Riviera,
Red Sardine Sauce

This dish conjures up memories of outdoor dining on the Riviera: blue skies, cypress trees, and a calming azure sea. Follow with a steamy bowl of fresh-cooked mussels and crusty garlic bread.

500 ml/16 fl oz crushed tomatoes in juice

250 ml/8 fl oz sardines in olive oil (skinless and boneless)

250 g/8 oz linguine pasta

In a large nonstick frying pan, heat the crushed tomatoes and juice. Add the sardines and their oil and cook over low heat 5 or 6 minutes, breaking up the sardines with a wooden spoon.

Bring a large pan of salted water to a boil. Add the pasta and cook until al dente.

Add 60 ml/2 fl oz pasta cooking water to the red sauce and a generous amount of freshly ground black pepper.

Drain the pasta well and serve with the hot tomato sauce on top. Makes 500 ml/16 fl oz sauce.

Serves 3 to 4

ADD-ONS
Add a handful of freshly chopped Italian parsley.

GRAPENOTE
Try something ultra-rustic from southern Italy or Sicily, like Aglianico del Vulture or Terrale Rosso.

Cheese Raviolini, Roasted Pumpkin Sauce

ADD-ONS

Thinly slice Pecorino Romano cheese (with peppercorns, if available) with a sharp cheese knife. Serve on top of the steamy bowl of pasta and sauce.

GRAPENOTE

Try a chardonnay with a touch of oak from California or Australia.

Pasta di zucca is a familiar dish in northern Italy. Here I use slow-roasted pumpkin as a delectable sauce for cheese-filled raviolini (little ravioli). Sprinkle with toasted pumpkin seeds for added crunch.

> **1 kg/2 lb fresh pumpkin or other winter squash**
>
> **500 ml/16 fl oz homemade chicken broth (page 96) or canned**
>
> **500 g/1 lb cheese raviolini (see Note)**

Preheat the oven to 200°C/400°F/gas 6.

Cut the pumpkin into several large pieces, removing any seeds or membrane. Reserve seeds if using for garnish (see Note). Place pumpkin in a baking tin, flesh side down, and pour 60 ml/2 fl oz water over the top. Bake for 1 hour, turning over after 30 minutes. The pumpkin will be lightly caramelized.

Meanwhile, reduce the chicken broth until you have 375 ml/12 fl oz. Keep warm.

Remove the pumpkin from the oven. Scrape the flesh from the skin and put in a blender or a food processor. Blend until very smooth, slowly adding the reduced broth. Taste the sauce, adding salt if needed. Keep warm.

Cook the raviolini in boiling salted water until tender. Drain well. Serve with the hot pumpkin sauce. Add coarsely ground black pepper to taste, or scatter with toasted pumpkin seeds.

Serves 5 to 6

Notes: Cheese raviolini are available in the refrigerated section of some supermarkets. If not use ravioli. To toast pumpkin seeds: Pour boiling water over seeds in a small bowl and steep for 30 minutes. Drain well and pat dry with kitchen paper. Bake on a baking tray in a 150°C/300°F/gas 2 oven for 25 minutes, then sprinkle with salt.

Hungarian Cabbage and Noodles

This was my comfort food when I was growing up with my beautiful Hungarian mother. Recently, I prowled Budapest looking for a version better than hers, but I never found one. You can also sauté some onion with the cabbage, as she often does.

1 large head white cabbage

250 g/4 oz unsalted butter

375 g/12 oz medium-wide egg noodles

With a sharp knife, shred the cabbage into 6-mm/¼-inch-wide slices. Place in a large bowl and sprinkle with salt. Cover with a plate to weight it down and refrigerate overnight. Put in a tin to collect any liquid. The next day, turn the cabbage out into a colander and squeeze dry.

In a large pan, melt the butter and add the cabbage. Sauté over medium heat until the cabbage is light brown and very soft, 30 to 40 minutes.

Cook the noodles according to the package directions. Drain the noodles and toss them with the cabbage, adding lots of freshly ground black pepper.

Serves 4

Slice 1 large onion very thin and sauté it with the cabbage. Sprinkle with caraway seeds.

GRAPENOTE

Serve with a chilled barrel-fermented sauvignon blanc from California. Or for a more sophisticated pairing, try a Hungarian Tokay with a degree of sweetness. Serve chilled.

Farfalle with Broccoli, Broccoli-Butter Sauce

ADD-ONS

Shower with julienned basil leaves.

GRAPENOTE

Try a dry chenin blanc from New Zealand, South Africa, Chile, or Argentina, or savour one of the semillon-chardonnay blends from Australia, like Wynns, or Trident, from Seaview Bay.

Although there are more than 600 shapes of pasta, some varieties have a special affinity for certain ingredients. Bowties and broccoli florets make a great-looking plate of food. Ingenuity turns the woody stems into a sublime sauce.

> 1 large head broccoli (500 g/1 lb)
>
> 250 g/8 oz farfalle (bowtie) pasta
>
> 45 g/1½ oz butter, cold

Cut the broccoli buds into small florets, leaving only 12 mm/½ inch of the stem. Reserve.

Peel the remaining stems and cut them into 2.5-cm/1-inch pieces. Cook in 300 ml/½ pint salted water for about 25 minutes, covered, in a small pan. When the stems are very soft, transfer the contents of the pan to a blender. Purée the stems and water until very smooth. Add the butter, cut in small pieces, and process. Add a little water if necessary to make a smooth sauce. Add salt and pepper to taste and transfer to a small pan.

Meanwhile, cook the pasta in a pan of salted boiling water for about 10 minutes. Add the broccoli florets to the pan and cook 3 to 4 minutes, until broccoli and pasta are tender.

Heat the sauce gently and pour over the drained pasta.

Serves 4 (about 300 ml/½ pint sauce)

Orecchiette with Chicory and Sun- Dried Tomatoes

Sun-dried tomatoes marinated in olive oil should become a staple in your pantry. They add a sweet acidity to dishes, and a Mediterranean spin. Tossed with orecchiette pasta ("little ears") and long strips of "chlorophyll-challenged" chicory, they make this a happening dish. Serve steaming on a big oval platter, sprinkled with tiny capers for company.

250 g/8 oz sun-dried tomatoes in oil

375 g/12 oz chicory (3 medium-to-large)

250 g/8 oz orecchiette pasta

Drain the oil from the tomatoes and place the oil in a large frying pan. Cut the tomatoes in half and add them to the oil. Slice the chicory into 6-mm/¼-inch-thick slices (hold the knife on the diagonal to make oval-shaped slices). Add to the oil. Cook over medium-high heat until the chicory is soft and the tomatoes are tender, about 10 minutes. Add salt and freshly ground black pepper to taste.

Meanwhile, cook the pasta for 12 to 15 minutes in boiling salted water or until done. Drain well. Put the pasta on a warm platter and cover thoroughly with sauce. Serve hot, or cold as a salad.

Serves 4

ADD-ONS

Scatter 1 tablespoon small capers on top of the sauce.

GRAPENOTE

Stylish with white or rosé: Try a viognier from the Rhône, or Rouvière Rosé or Bandol Rosé from Provence.

Angel's Food
I and II

Cappellini, also known as angel's hair, are long superfine strands of pasta available both dried and fresh. I like to use fresh cappellini to toss with saline black caviar, and dried cappellini to bathe in truffle oil. This is truly the "food of the gods."

I. Angel Hair Pasta with Caviar

375 g/12 oz fresh angel hair pasta

90 g/3 oz unsalted butter

125 ml/4 fl oz sevruga or osetra caviar

Boil the pasta in a large pan of salted water. Cook until just tender but not soft. This should take only about 2 minutes. Drain in a colander.

Meanwhile, melt the butter gently, being careful not to let it brown.

Put the pasta in a large, warm bowl. Pour the hot melted butter over the pasta. Toss. Add the caviar and toss again. Serve immediately.

Serves 4 to 6

ADD-ONS

Add a few drops of fresh lemon juice or garnish with a long strip of lemon zest, gently twisted.

GRAPENOTE

Only a glass of weighty champagne will do. How about nonvintage Bollinger or, since you're splurging, Dom Pérignon or Krug?

II. Angel Hair Pasta with Truffle Oil

250 g/8 oz dried angel hair pasta

**3 tablespoons truffle oil—plus additional for
drizzling if desired**

60 g/2 oz grated Parmigiano-Reggiano

Bring a large pan of salted water to a boil. Add the pasta and cook until tender, about 8 minutes, being careful not to overcook. Drain the pasta in a colander, saving 60 ml/2 fl oz of the cooking water. Put the pasta in a warmed ceramic bowl.

Add the truffle oil, a little cooking water, salt to taste, and a generous amount of freshly ground white pepper. Toss gently, adding a little more cooking water if necessary.

Divide the pasta evenly into soup plates. Sprinkle each with 2 tablespoons cheese. Do not mix. Drizzle with a little additional truffle oil, if desired.

Serves 4

GRAPENOTE

This deserves a great Tuscan red like Sassicaia, but it also would be quite thrilling with a weighty Italian white like Mastroberardino's Greco di Tufo.

A Very Old Neapolitan Recipe: Macaroni and Tomatoes

ADD-ONS

Add 30 g/1 oz freshly grated Parmigiano-Reggiano to the hot pasta and toss.

GRAPENOTE

Try a bottle of Chianti Classico from a favourite producer.

Time lends enchantment to many dishes. This recipe was found by Italian cooking master Giuliano Bugialli in an Italian cookbook from 1841. Naples is famous as the home of the pizza, but it's also the home of this fascinating pasta. Giuliano suggests a short tubular pasta, but I like the charm of cavatelli.

250 g/8 oz dried cavatelli

6 tablespoons olive oil

1 (880-g/28-oz) can imported plum tomatoes in juice

Preheat the oven to 200°C/400°F/gas 6.

In a medium bowl, mix the pasta and the olive oil. Let the pasta soak in the oil for 20 minutes.

Add tomatoes and juice to pasta. Add 1 teaspoon coarse salt and freshly ground black pepper to taste and mix well.

Transfer the pasta to a large, shallow casserole brushed with a little olive oil. Bake 45 minutes, mixing several times during baking to prevent the pasta from sticking to casserole. Serve immediately.

Serves 2 to 3

Spinach Fettuccine with Tomato Butter

Never did such a little tube produce a big sauce with such tomatoey intensity. This takes only minutes to make and will become your favourite emergency meal.

185 g/6 oz good-quality tomato purée

250 g/4 oz unsalted butter

375 g/12 oz fresh spinach fettuccine

Put the tomato purée in a heavy small saucepan and add 60 ml/2 fl oz water. Heat gently. Cut the butter into small pieces and add to the tomato mixture. Stir with a wooden spoon over low heat until the butter is incorporated. Season with salt and pepper to taste.

In a large pan of boiling water, cook the spinach fettuccine until it is tender. This will take only a few minutes. Do not overcook. Drain in a colander, saving 3 tablespoons of cooking liquid. Add the reserved cooking water to the tomato sauce and heat gently.

Place the pasta on a large, warm platter and spoon the hot tomato sauce over the top.

Serves 4

Add freshly grated Grana Padano on top of the pasta. Grana Padano is a cheese similar to Parmigiano-Reggiano made near Parma.

Penne and Pencil Asparagus, Torta di Mascarpone

ADD-ONS

Garnish with julienned basil or lightly toasted pine nuts.

GRAPENOTE

This dish can handle a variety of wine partners, white or red. Try an assertive sauvignon blanc from Italy, or a bright young nebbiolo from the Valtellina region.

This is one of the first dishes I created using only three ingredients. Its delicious simplicity led to the development of an entire new repertoire of recipes.

Small cubes of torta di mascarpone—a layered loaf of mascarpone, provolone, and basil—melt miraculously into a creamy, flavourful sauce. You can find it in specialist cheese shops.

> 250 g/8 oz penne
>
> 250 g/8 oz thin asparagus, cut on the diagonal into 3-cm/1¼-inch lengths
>
> 375 g/12 oz torta di mascarpone, cut into small pieces

Bring a large pan of salted water to a boil. Add the penne and cook 8 minutes, or until it is just beginning to get tender. Add the asparagus pieces and cook 2 minutes, or until the asparagus and the pasta are both al dente. Drain the pasta well, saving 80 ml/3 fl oz of the cooking water.

Put the hot cooking water in the bottom of a large warmed bowl. Add the drained pasta and asparagus. Add the torta di mascarpone and stir gently with a wooden spoon until the cheese melts completely. Season with salt and freshly ground pepper to taste.

Serves 4

Chapter 9

Main Courses

Once upon a time the word "gourmet" referred to those apt to judge a meal for its elaborateness rather than by the quality of its food. One of the goals of *Recipes 1-2-3* is to redefine the gourmet as one who demands quality and respects the clarity of simple flavours.

Especially when it comes to the heart of the meal.

Although strongly infused with the flavours of the Mediterranean (my style of cooking for over a decade), these main courses reflect the hybridization of the modern kitchen—where the exotic becomes familiar and sophistication becomes comfortable.

Steamed Clams in Thyme Butter

I ate this memorable dish while on a consulting trip to Paris. Restaurant Le Duc on Boulevard Raspail was known for its all-seafood menu, impressive with its selection of twenty-six fish main courses and more than a dozen choices of crustaceans. My favourite: Poulardes Sautées au Thym.

ADD-ONS

Serve with small steamed red potatoes or with garlic bread.

GRAPENOTE

Classic with a bottle of chilled Muscadet "Sur Lie" or Picpoul de Pinet, a crisp white wine that is enormously popular in Paris.

about 5 dozen clams

250 g/4 oz unsalted butter

1 large bunch fresh thyme

Scrub the clams well and wash them thoroughly. Soak them in a cold brine of 60 g/2 oz salt to 1 gallon of water for 30 minutes. Wash again.

Melt the butter in a large heavy pan with a tightly fitting cover. Add 125 ml/4 fl oz water, 3 tablespoons fresh thyme leaves, 1 teaspoon whole black peppercorns, and 1½ teaspoons coarse salt. Add the clams, cover and cook over high heat 6 to 8 minutes, until shells open. Shake pan back and forth to cook clams evenly.

Remove from the heat the moment the shells open. Pour the clams, shells and broth into heated bowls. Serve immediately.

Serves 4 to 6

Barbecue Pepper Prawns

This is a New Orleans–style recipe that has nothing to do with an outdoor barbecue. Serve with Bay-Smoked Potatoes (page 195) or chilli-spiked pasta for a great flavour match.

1 kg/2 lb large prawns, in their shells

250 g/8 oz butter, cold, cut into small pieces

3 tablespoons Worcestershire sauce

Preheat the oven to 200°C/400°F/gas 6.

Wash the prawns and peel them, leaving the tails on. Make a cut along the back of each prawn and rinse under cold water to remove the vein. Dry on kitchen paper.

Place the prawns in a single layer in a shallow casserole with 15 g/½ oz crushed black peppercorns. Top with the butter. Bake 5 minutes.

Toss the prawns, then add the Worcestershire sauce and 2 teaspoons coarse salt. Bake 2 minutes longer.

Put under the grill for 1 minute. Remove and serve in soup plates with the pan juices.

Serves 5 to 6

ADD-ONS

Squeeze the juice of 2 lemons over the top.

GRAPENOTE

Try an aggressively varietal sauvignon blanc from South Africa, like Thelema— or Brander, from the Santa Ynez area of California.

Tuna Burgers, Hoisin and Pickled Ginger Root

GRAPENOTE

This is a nice match with a not-too-sweet American wine. Try chilled white zinfandel from Dunnewood Vineyards, or Vin de Mistral Grenache Rosé from Joseph Phelps.

At the Rainbow Room restaurant in New York, where I am consulting chef, members of the Rockefeller Center Club have been eating tuna burgers with great relish. Or rather, with pickled ginger root. They like it seared rare, sitting on a bed of spicy gingered coleslaw. No one asks for ketchup . . . or even a hamburger bun!

1 kg/2 lb fresh tuna, skin and bones removed

6 tablespoons hoisin sauce

**6 tablespoons Japanese pickled ginger root,
kimchee or Red Onion Salad (page 132)**

Mince the tuna very fine with a sharp knife, or grind it in a meat grinder (you can ask your fishmonger to do this). The tuna should resemble minced meat. Season with 1½ teaspoons coarse salt and freshly ground black pepper to taste. Form into 6 thick patties. Chill until ready to use.

Heat the hoisin sauce in a small saucepan with 2 tablespoons water. Keep warm.

Preheat the grill. Grill the tuna burgers on both sides until the outside is browned and the inside is pink, about 6 minutes total.

Pour the warm sauce over the tuna and garnish with pickled ginger root, kimchee or Red Onion Salad. Serve with a knife and fork.

Serves 6

Red Snapper in Burnt Orange Oil

I use every edible part of the orange in this dish: juice—which emulsifies into a sauce—the segments for texture, and the peel for a heady aroma. These flavours enliven the sweet, fresh red snapper fillets, with dazzling results.

5 medium juice oranges, or blood oranges if available

125 ml/4 fl oz olive oil or herb-flavoured oil (basil, page 156, rosemary, sage)

4 red snapper fillets, 185 g/6 oz each, skin removed

Wash the oranges. With a vegetable peeler, remove 8 long strips of orange zest and reserve. Make sure to remove any white pith. Cut the rind completely off 4 oranges. Cut the oranges between the membranes to make segments, being careful to remove all membrane. Reserve.

Heat the oil in large nonstick frying pan. Add the strips of orange zest. Just as they become dark brown, remove and reserve.

Sprinkle salt and pepper on both sides of the fish. Add to the hot oil and sauté on both sides until crisp and lightly browned (you may need to do this in two batches). Remove the cooked fish to a warm platter.

Add the orange segments and the juice of the remaining orange (just cut in half and squeeze) to the oil in the pan. Cook over high heat for 1 minute, add salt and pepper to taste, and pour over the fish. Garnish with the burnt orange peel.

Serves 4

In the oil in the pan, fry paper-thin slices of raw carrot (sliced lengthwise) until crisp. Serve with the fish.

GRAPENOTE

Open a bottle of chardonnay from Australia—Rosemount Estate or Lindemans—or Beringer reserve from California.

Crispy Salmon with Pancetta and Sage

ADD-ONS

Drinking red? Try White Polenta with Parmigiano-Reggiano (page 189). Drinking white? Serve with Chardonnay Cabbage (page 198) or Potato-Fennel Mash (page 190).

GRAPENOTES

The full meaty flavour of the fish will go beautifully with a chardonnay or a medium-bodied pinot noir with a hint of spice and oak in its finish.

Red wine with fish? You bet. This sophisticated confluence of flavours makes the much-loved salmon worthy of a great pinot noir. White wine with fish? Yes! A big chardonnay, if you serve this crispy salmon on a bed of buttery braised cabbage.

4 thick salmon fillets, 185 g/6 oz each, cut from the centre of fish

250 g/8 oz thinly sliced pancetta

24 leaves fresh sage

Remove the skin and with tweezers all the small bones from the salmon. Holding a sharp knife on the bias, cut 2 deep slits across the width of each piece of fish. Do not cut all the way through. You will have 2 "pockets" in each piece.

Lay the pancetta flat in a large nonstick frying pan. Cook over low heat until most of fat is rendered and the pancetta is just beginning to crisp. Remove the pancetta with tongs and let it cool 5 minutes. Reserve the rendered fat.

Place the pancetta and 3 sage leaves in each slit, allowing the edges of the sage and pancetta to show. Heat the fat in a frying pan. Season the fish with salt and pepper and place, slit side down, in the frying pan. Cook over medium heat until the fish begins to brown and get crisp. Turn the fillets and finish cooking to desired doneness. The fish should be crisp on the outside, moist on the inside.

Serves 4

Roast Cod with Red Pepper Purée

You might use roasted fresh peppers for this dish with good results, but I love the tingle of vinegar in the sauce, so I keep a jar of roasted red peppers (pimientos) on my shelf for a luxurious and quick dish. Buy thick, fleshy cod fillets.

> 4 cod fillets, 185 g/6 oz each
>
> 1 (375-g/12-oz) jar of roasted red peppers (pimientos)
>
> 60 g/2 oz unsalted butter, cold

Preheat the oven to 190°C/375°F/gas 5.

Dust the cod fillets with salt and freshly ground white pepper. Set aside.

Purée the roasted peppers with their liquid in a food processor until smooth and thick. Transfer to a small, heavy pan.

In large, ovenproof frying pan melt 7 g/¼ oz of the butter. Sauté the fish briefly on each side and put it in the oven for 8 to 10 minutes. When it's done, the fish will flake easily, but do not overcook.

Heat the red pepper purée until very hot. Remove from the heat. Whisk in the remaining cold butter and stir until smooth (sauce yields about 375 ml/12 fl oz). Keep warm.

Remove the fish from the oven, pour any juices into the red pepper sauce, and mix.

Pool 80 ml/3 fl oz sauce on the bottom of each plate. Place the fish on top.

Serves 4

ADD-ONS

Serve with Braised Celery Batons, Fried Celery Leaves (page 204).

GRAPENOTE

Lovely match with an Anjou Blanc from the Loire Valley to balance the sweetness and acidity in the dish.

Rosemary-Infused Swordfish

Swordfish has a special affinity for rosemary and garlic. In addition to its very Mediterranean flavours, this dish is a low-calorie joy, because it dry-cooks in the pan. Use ultra-fresh fish.

2 large cloves garlic, very finely minced

2 tablespoons fresh rosemary, finely minced

750 g/1½ lb swordfish, cut into 4 steaks

In a small bowl, mix the garlic, 1½ teaspoons coarse ground black pepper, 1½ teaspoons coarse salt, and the rosemary until you have a coarse paste. A pestle and mortar is ideal. Spread the mixture evenly on both sides of the fish. Let sit 1 hour.

Heat a nonstick frying pan or grill pan until hot. Cook the swordfish 3 to 4 minutes over medium-high heat on each side until browned and lightly caramelized.

Serves 4

ADD-ONS

You can add 2 tablespoons olive oil while the fish is marinating, or drizzle extra-virgin olive oil on top of the fish after cooking. Pass fresh lemon wedges and garnish with fresh rosemary sprigs. Delicious with Cumin-Scented Couscous (page 212) and Slow-Roasted Plum Tomatoes (page 220).

GRAPENOTES

A special match with viognier, provençal white Cassis, or a more unusual Châteauneuf-du-Pape Blanc from France.

Pepper-Seared Tuna, Cool Mango Relish

Sales of fish and seafood have risen considerably in the last ten years. But just wait until people start eating this dish—mango sales will also soar! Together these flavours are a singular sensation.

2 ripe mangoes

6 tablespoons chopped fresh coriander, plus whole leaves for garnish

4 fresh tuna steaks, 185 g/6 oz each

About 1 hour before serving, peel the mangoes with a sharp knife. Cut the flesh away from the stone, dice it into 6-mm/¼-inch pieces, and put it in a small bowl. Add the chopped coriander and a pinch of salt and mix well. Chill for 30 minutes.

Lightly press ½ teaspoon coarse ground black pepper into one side of each tuna steak. Sprinkle lightly with salt. Place the fish, pepper side down, in a large nonstick frying pan. Cook on both sides over medium-high heat until the fish is seared on the outside but still pink in the centre. Cut the tuna on the bias with a sharp knife into 12-mm/½-inch-thick slices.

Mound mango relish in the centre of each plate. Arrange the tuna slices, overlapping, to form a circle around the relish. Garnish with fresh coriander leaves.

Serves 4

ADD-ONS

Serve with wedges of fresh lime. Also delicious atop Red Onion Salad (page 132).

GRAPENOTE

The appealing fruit, perfume, and acidity of the South African sauvignon blanc from Mulderbosch makes this fish dish sing.

Red Onion Salad

This sprightly onion salad is one of the most enticing relishes I've ever had. It's the balance of vinegar and sweetness that makes my mouth water. Toss with 1 kg/2 lb large chilled prawns for a fabulous first course. Or serve on top of salads, sandwiches, grilled fish, poultry, steaks . . .

>   500 g/1 lb medium-size red onions
>   250 ml/8 fl oz tarragon vinegar
>   125 g/4 oz sugar

Peel the onions, slice them into 6-mm/¼-inch-thick rings, and put them in a large jar. Pour in 250 ml/8 fl oz water, the vinegar, the sugar, ½ teaspoon black peppercorns and ¼ teaspoon coarse salt. Cover tightly and shake well until the sugar is dissolved. Store in the refrigerator. Let marinate, refrigerated, one day before serving.

Makes 750 ml/24 fl oz

Steamed Halibut,
Sweet Pepper Confetti

Halibut is known as "the hippo of the sea." I'm especially fond of the way the brightly coloured peppers contrast with the snowy whiteness of the fish.

> 2 each: yellow and red sweet peppers
>
> 60 ml/2 fl oz olive oil or Garlic Oil (page 52),
> plus 2 tablespoons for oiling the fish
>
> 4 halibut steaks, 185 g/6 oz each

To make the sweet pepper confetti: Cut the peppers meticulously into little 8-mm/⅓-inch squares. Place them in a small nonstick frying pan with the 60 ml/2 fl oz oil. Add ½ teaspoon coarse salt and ¼ teaspoon whole black peppercorns. Cover and simmer over very low heat for 10 minutes, or until the peppers are tender.

Brush the halibut with a little oil and season with salt and freshly ground white pepper. Steam in a large pan fitted with a steamer basket until the fish is cooked to the desired degree of doneness—about 10 minutes, depending on thickness. Pour "confetti" over the fish and serve immediately.

Serves 4

ADD-ONS

Serve with lemon wedges. Shower with julienned basil or flat parsley. Or add 1 teaspoon fennel seed to the peppers while cooking.

GRAPENOTE

These clean flavours call for a medium-bodied white with well-balanced acidity. Try a chardonnay with finesse, either from California or Italy. Also great with Pinot d'Alsace from Domaine Zind-Humbrecht.

Salmon Baked in Vine Leaves

Oh, is this good! Salmon baked in an ancestral "wrap" of briny vine leaves, softened with a bit of butter. Keep the vine leaves on the fish when you serve it—they are delicious. This is pure Med-Rim when served with Fried Lemon and Courgette Salad. It is also a wonderful way to prepare halibut fillets.

4 thick salmon fillets, 185 g/6 oz each, cut from the centre of the fish

75 g/2½ oz unsalted butter

8 large vine leaves in brine

Preheat the oven to 230°C/450°F/gas 8.

Remove the skin and any bones from the fish. Season well with salt and pepper. Slice the butter thinly and place 7 g/¼ oz on top of each fillet.

Remove the vine leaves from their brine and pat dry with kitchen paper. Wrap the fish tightly in vine leaves, using 2 for each piece of fish. Tuck in the ends of the vine leaves to make a tight, neat package.

Spread 30 g/1 oz of the remaining butter over the bottom of a baking tin. Use bits of the remaining butter to cover the tops of the vine leaf–wrapped fish.

Put the fish on the baking tray and bake 8 minutes. Serve the fish immediately, still wrapped in the vine leaves.

Serves 4

Pan-Seared Tuna Niçoise, Tomato "Water"

A chic version of the more traditional salade niçoise, this is made with fresh rosy-pink tuna topped with a salad of julienned tomato and oil-cured olives—the signature components. Natural tomato juices become the dressing. Serve with Parmesan Lace Galettes and you'll have a riot of flavours, textures and temperatures.

> **6 large, ripe tomatoes**
>
> **36 oil-cured black olives**
>
> **4 fresh tuna steaks, 185 g/6 oz each**

One to two hours before serving, trim off the outer wall of the tomatoes with a small, sharp knife. Remove the pulp from inside the tomato and reserve. Cut the wall into thin julienned strips 3 mm/⅛ inch wide by 4 cm/1½ inches long. Stone the olives and cut them in half. Put the tomato julienne and olives in a small bowl with ½ teaspoon coarse salt. Let sit for 30 minutes at room temperature.

Coarsely chop the reserved pulp of the tomatoes, removing any seeds. Put in a blender at high speed and process until you have a smooth purée. Reserve.

Sprinkle the tuna lightly with white pepper and salt. Heat a large nonstick frying pan and sear the tuna on both sides until browned but still pink inside.

Spoon the tomato water on the bottom of 4 large plates. Place the cooked fish on sauce and top with the tomato-olive mixture.

Serves 4

ADD-ONS

Garnish with finely chopped egg white. Serve with thinly sliced Bay-Smoked Potatoes (page 195) and steamed haricots verts. Or serve with Parmesan Lace Galettes (page 49).

GRAPENOTE

Try a well-chilled off-dry rosé like Tavel, or a white Bordeaux such as Château Bonnet, to complement this dish's sunny flavours.

Two-Way Salmon and Courgettes

Three simple ingredients can make two dramatically different styles of fish: poached and pan-seared, plus two "gourmet" sauces: a dark courgette coulis and a creamy courgette butter sauce.

GRAPENOTE

Serve with a full-bodied California chardonnay or French white Burgundy. From California, try Château Woltner—from France, a Montagny.

I. Poached Salmon with Courgettes, Two Sauces

750 g/1½ lb medium-size courgettes

4 salmon fillets, 185 g/6 oz each

30 g/1 oz unsalted butter, cold

Cut one-sixth of the courgettes into paper-thin rounds. Place in an overlapping pattern on top of the fish. Sprinkle with salt and freshly ground white pepper and wrap each piece tightly in cling film. Refrigerate 30 minutes.

Cut the remaining courgettes in half lengthwise and then across into 12-mm/½-inch pieces. Put in a medium-size pan with 125 ml/ 4 fl oz water and ½ teaspoon salt. Bring to a boil, lower the heat, cover, and cook 15 minutes, or until the courgettes are very soft.

Meanwhile, unwrap the salmon and poach in a shallow pan in 2.5 cm/1 inch of water until cooked through. (You can also steam the fish in the cling film in a steamer.)

Transfer one-half of the cooked courgettes and one-half of the cooking liquid to a blender and purée until smooth. Reserve. Transfer remaining courgettes and liquid to the blender and purée until smooth. Add the butter and purée until thick and creamy.

You will now have two sauces—a dark-green coulis (with no butter) and a light, creamy sauce with butter.

To serve, place 60 ml/2 fl oz of the dark sauce on the bottom of each of 4 plates. Top each with a warm poached salmon fillet and put 2 tablespoons of the buttery sauce over the top of each.

II Pan-Seared Salmon, Creamy Courgette Sauce

250 g/8 oz courgettes

4 salmon fillets, 185 g/6 oz each

30 g/1 oz unsalted butter, cold, cut into a few pieces

Cut the courgettes into large chunks and put in a small pan. Cook in 60 ml/2 fl oz water with ¼ teaspoon salt until very soft.

Meanwhile, season the salmon with salt and pepper and sear in a nonstick frying pan on both sides until medium-rare. Keep warm.

As soon as the courgettes are soft, transfer the contents of the pan to a blender. Blend until smooth and creamy. Add the butter. Blend again—sauce will lighten in colour and thicken. Add salt and pepper to taste. Pour the hot sauce immediately around the salmon.

I, II: Serves 4

GRAPENOTES

Because you have seared the fish, this preparation will lend itself beautifully to a lighter-style pinot noir, or a cru Beaujolais.

Perfect Chicken Salad

Once you use this method of poaching whole chicken, you will never make it any other way, for the meat has a remarkable velvety texture. As a bonus, you can reduce the broth to use as a base for restorative chicken soup. Cut the chicken into small dice for sandwiches; julienne into long, thin strips for main-course salads.

1.25-kg/2½-lb whole chicken

250 g/8 oz chopped celery

250 ml/8 fl oz mayonnaise or Flavoured Mayonnaise (page 139)

Wash and clean the chicken. Bring 4 litres/6½ pints of water to boil in a large pan. Submerge the chicken and boil quietly, uncovered, for 15 minutes.

Turn off the heat, cover, and let the chicken remain in the water for 30 minutes.

Remove from the water and reserve the broth for another use. Pull out as many bones as possible and refrigerate the chicken until cold. Remove all bones and skin. Cut chicken into 12-mm/½-inch chunks.

Toss with the celery and mayonnaise. Chill. Makes about 1 kg/2 lb.

Serves 6

ADD-ONS

Serve on a platter lined with soft green lettuce, together with Red Onion Salad (page 132) and ripe cherry tomatoes.

GRAPENOTE

Try a chilled dry riesling or an easy-drinking dry chenin blanc.

Flavoured Mayonnaises I-II-III

I. Anchovy-Lemon Mayonnaise

250 ml/8 fl oz low calorie mayonnaise
1 (60-g/2-oz) can anchovies and capers in oil
Grated zest of 1 lemon and 1 tablespoon of lemon juice

Process all the ingredients in a blender until very smooth and creamy.
Add freshly ground black pepper to taste.

II. Sun-Dried Tomato Mayonnaise

250 ml/8 fl oz low calorie mayonnaise
60 ml/2 fl oz sun-dried tomatoes in oil
1 clove garlic, pushed through a garlic press

Put all the ingredients in a food processor and purée until smooth and
creamy. Add freshly ground black pepper to taste.

III. Spicy Coriander Mayonnaise

250 ml/8 fl oz low calorie mayonnaise
2½ tablespoons finely chopped fresh coriander
1 tablespoon minced pickled jalapeños

Combine all the ingredients in a small bowl and whisk until blended.

Each makes about 250 ml/8 fl oz

Chicken Roasted in a Salt Crust

Copious amounts of coarse salt form an impenetrable crust around the chicken in this dish, sealing in the natural juices and producing meltingly tender meat. Crack open the oven-baked igloo and herbal perfume will waft through your kitchen. Surprisingly, this ancient cooking method imparts a unique taste without excessive saltiness and is equally good (and dramatic) with whole red snapper.

> 1 whole 2-kg/4-lb chicken, at room
>   temperature
>
> Large bunch fresh thyme (enough to fill the
>   cavity of the chicken)
>
> 12 small new potatoes

Preheat the oven to 230°C/450°F/gas 8.

Wash the chicken and pat dry with kitchen paper. Fill the cavity with thyme and season the skin with freshly ground black pepper.

Pour 500 g/1 lb salt into the bottom of a deep ovenproof casserole or a pan with cover. Put the chicken on the salt, breast side up, and ring with the potatoes. Add salt to cover the top of the chicken (about 1.75 kg/3½ lb). Sprinkle with 250 ml/8 fl oz water, patting the salt down to make a solid crust.

Bake, covered, for 45 minutes. Remove the cover and bake 20 minutes more. Remove from the oven and let rest 10 minutes.

Crack the salt crust with the back of a heavy knife. Remove the chicken and potatoes. Remove all the salt with a pastry brush or kitchen paper. Cut the chicken as desired. Serve with sprigs of thyme and the roasted new potatoes.

Serves 4 to 6

ADD-ONS

Before baking, rub the skin of the chicken with 2 cloves of garlic that have been pushed through a garlic press. Serve the chicken drizzled with 60 ml/ 2 fl oz fruity olive oil that has been gently warmed.

GRAPENOTE

Try a simple Mâcon or Saint-Veran if you want white, or a Beaujolais-Villages if you want red.

Poulet Rôti with Wild Mushrooms

Nothing is more satisfying than a classic roast chicken, and this version, sauced with woodsy porcini mushrooms, rules the roost.

> 1 whole 2-kg/4-lb chicken
>
> 45 g/1½ oz dried porcini mushrooms
>
> 60 g/2 oz unsalted butter, cold

Preheat the oven to 190°C/375°F/gas 5.

Wash the chicken and pat it dry with kitchen paper. Save the neck and gizzards, except for the liver. Salt and pepper the chicken evenly and sprinkle salt and pepper in the cavity.

Soak the dried porcini in 500 ml/16 fl oz of very hot water for 20 minutes. Drain them, saving the soaking water. Sauté the mushrooms in 15 g/½ oz of the butter for 3 to 4 minutes. Fill the cavity of the chicken with the sautéed mushrooms. Truss the chicken and rub it with a tablespoon of butter. Place the chicken in a heavy, shallow casserole and roast for 1 to 1¼ hours, basting often.

Meanwhile, put the gizzards and the neck in a small pan with 125 ml/4 fl oz water and the mushroom liquid, strained through a fine sieve. Bring to a boil, lower the heat, and simmer 20 to 25 minutes, until the liquid is reduced to 300 ml/½ pint. Pour the liquid through a sieve and discard the gizzards and neck.

Remove chicken from the oven, untruss, and put on a platter. Scoop the mushrooms out of the chicken and put them in the roasting tin with the reduced mushroom juices. Reduce by one-third. Add salt and pepper to taste and whisk in 30 g/1 oz cold butter until the sauce emulsifies. Cut the chicken as desired and cover with the wild mushroom sauce.

Serves 4 to 6

Add 60 ml/2 fl oz ruby port to the juices in the roasting tin while reducing. A wonderful accompaniment to this classic preparation is Gratin Dauphinoise (page 192).

GRAPENOTE

A velvety, easy-drinking merlot would be a lovely way to integrate the flavours and body of this dish. If white is more to your liking, now's a good time to remember what great Burgundy is all about.

Country-Fried Chicken

When at the age of twenty-three I was first chef to New York's Mayor Ed Koch, "Hizzoner" selected the menu for my cooking debut, a dinner party for the Council of East Coast Mayors. Green salad, fried chicken, chocolate mousse. Little did I know this was the unofficial beginning of Recipes 1-2-3.

2 frying chickens, cut into eight pieces each

875 g/1¼ lb self-raising flour

500 g/1 lb vegetable lard

Put the chicken parts in a large bowl. Fill with cold water and refrigerate overnight (or for 12 hours). Pat the chicken pieces completely dry and lightly salt each piece. Mix the flour with 1 tablespoon freshly ground black pepper. Dredge each piece in the flour-pepper mixture.

Heat 250 g/8 oz of the lard in each of two large heavy frying pans. Add the chicken pieces, skin side down, and fry for 10 minutes. Cover and fry for 10 minutes more. Adjust the heat during cooking so the chicken continues to sizzle without spattering. Turn the chicken, cover and cook 10 more minutes. Turn the chicken again and cook uncovered 5 minutes, or until the chicken is crisp and the juices run clear.

Serves 8

ADD-ONS

Add a pinch of cinnamon, thyme, or nutmeg to the flour. Instead of water, you can soak the chicken in buttermilk. Or double-dip: After the first dip in seasoned flour, dip in the buttermilk, then in the flour again. Serve with green Tabasco.

GRAPENOTE

Choose a delightful chenin blanc. I also like a fruity red wine, such as dolcetto or young Chianti, for an upbeat contrast and a good way to cut through the fat.

Chicken-in-a-Watermelon

Fairly sweet and succulent, this improbable dish will make a big hit on April Fools' Day, which is strangely bereft of a single signature dish. It makes a spectacular, if fairly alarming, presentation on a silver tray.

1 very large watermelon

Roasting chicken, 2.5 to 3 kg/5 to 6 lb

1 tablespoon five-spice powder

Preheat the oven to 200°C/400°F/gas 6.

Cut a 6-mm/¼-inch-thick horizontal slice off one long side of the watermelon and discard it. Cut off the top third of the melon horizontally. Core and seed both parts of the melon, making room for the chicken. Season the cavity of chicken with salt and freshly ground black pepper. Rub the skin of chicken with the five-spice powder.

Place the chicken in the larger portion of the melon and then place the other piece of melon on top, securing it with long skewers. Put a baking tin on the bottom rack of the oven to catch any juices. Bake the watermelon directly on the rack above for 2 hours, then reduce the oven to 150°C/300°F/gas 2 and bake for 2½ hours longer.

Very carefully place the watermelon on a tray and present it to your guests. Return to the kitchen to remove the chicken from the watermelon and carve it. Remove the juices from the watermelon and reduce them in a frying pan until thickened.

Serves 6 to 8

ADD-ONS

Whisk 45 g/1½ oz cold unsalted butter into juices while reducing them in the frying pan. For extra flavour, add 1 tablespoon fresh lemon juice or soy sauce.

GRAPENOTE

A remarkable contrast with a not-too-sweet white zinfandel from California.

Chicken "Villagio," Diced Lemon Sauce

ADD-ONS

Garnish with julienned basil leaves or strips of roasted red or yellow pepper.

GRAPENOTE

Perfect with San Anselmi, a single-vineyard soave, or Vernaccia di San Gimignano, if you're drinking white; or try a Montepulciano d'Abruzzo if you're drinking red.

This inventive, rustic dish is characterized by strong, definitive flavours. Italians would serve it with la scarpetta ("the slipper"), a piece of bread for mopping up the delicious juices. Accompany with creamy White Polenta with Parmigiano-Reggiano (page 189) and a sturdy Italian wine.

8 chicken thighs (about 1.25 kg/2½ lb)

3 medium-size lemons

185 g/6 oz pepperoni (2.5-cm/1-inch-diameter sausage)

Trim any excess fat from the chicken. Put the chicken in a ceramic bowl. Grate the zest of the two lemons on the medium-size holes of a hand grater. Save the lemons. Add the rind to the chicken, along with ½ teaspoon coarse salt and ¼ teaspoon coarse ground black pepper. Slice the pepperoni into 6-mm/¼-inch-thick rounds. Add to the chicken, mix well, and marinate several hours or overnight.

Cut the pith away from the lemons with a sharp knife. Make sure all of the white membrane is removed. Cut lemon flesh into 6-mm/¼-inch dice. Reserve.

Put the chicken, skin side down, in a large nonstick frying pan, along with pepperoni. Cook over medium heat until the chicken is golden and turn over. Continue to cook and turn until the chicken is done and the sausage is browned. This will take about 20 minutes. Add the diced lemon and continue to cook, 3 to 4 minutes more. The lemon will thicken the pan juices. Add salt and pepper to taste.

Transfer to a large platter with a slotted spoon. Serve piping hot.

Serves 4

Yogurt Chicken with Blackened Onions

The onion-and-yogurt marinade tenderizes chicken to satiny perfection. For an unusual flavour match, try this with Barley-Buttermilk Salad, flecked with coriander. This dish feels like summer.

8 chicken thighs (about1.25 kg/2½ lb)

375 ml/12 fl oz natural yogurt

185 g/6 oz chopped onions

Remove any excess fat from the chicken. Put the chicken in a medium non-metallic bowl with the yogurt and diced onions. Add ½ teaspoon salt and mix well. Cover and refrigerate overnight.

Preheat the oven to 180°C/350°F/gas 4.

Place the chicken pieces in a metal baking tin, making sure the pieces are separated and well covered with yogurt and onions. Bake for 40 minutes. Then grill the chickens, with the tin set at the greatest distance from heat, until onions are somewhat blackened. Be careful not to let them burn completely. This will take 4 to 5 minutes. Sprinkle with ½ teaspoon salt. Serve hot or cold.

Serves 4

ADD-ONS

Serve with Barley-Buttermilk Salad (page 194). Shower with freshly chopped coriander or ground sumac.

GRAPENOTE

An interesting and refreshing match with a rosé wine.

Poussin Under a Brick

You really need a brick or two for making this dish, because the authentic northern Italian preparation, mattone *(the word for heavy brick), requires that the poussin lie completely flat while cooking. Ultra-crisp skin and succulent meat will have you licking your fingers.*

750-kg/1½-lb poussin

3 tablespoons Garlic Oil (page 52)—plus additional for drizzling, if desired

125 ml/4 fl oz dry white wine

With kitchen shears, cut the poussin along the length of the backbone. With your fist, pound the bird flat so that it is butterflied. Season with salt and pepper.

Heat the oil in a large nonstick frying pan. Place the poussin, skin side down, in the oil and place a brick wrapped in foil on top. Cook over medium heat, turning every 2 to 3 minutes, for 10 minutes, or until golden brown.

Remove the bird to a large warm plate. Add the wine to the pan and reduce over high heat, scraping up the browned bits in the pan. When the sauce has thickened, pour it over the poussin. Serve immediately. Drizzle with additional garlic oil if desired.

Serves 1 or 2

ADD-ONS

Add 1 tablespoon chopped fresh rosemary to the pan while reducing the wine.

GRAPENOTE

Try a Dolcetto d'Alba for an authentic flavour match, or drink the white wine you've cooked with—perhaps an Italian pinot grigio from Bollini or a white from Orvieto.

Brine-Cured Poussins,
Glazed Shallots and Parsnip Purée

This 1-2-3 dish is actually three recipes in one. Soaking these small birds (a breed of baby chicken) in brine makes them particularly moist and brings out their flavour. This is a lovely dish for entertaining, especially when autumn is in the air.

2 poussins, 625 g/1¼ lb

16 medium-size shallots

500 g/1 lb parsnips

Wash the poussins and sprinkle the cavities with salt. Place them in a large bowl or plastic bucket and cover with cold water. Add 185 g/ 6 oz salt and stir until the salt dissolves. Refrigerate for 6 hours, but not longer.

Parboil shallots for 5 minutes, then peel.

Preheat the oven to 180°C/350°F/gas 4.

Remove the poussins from the brine and pat them dry with kitchen paper. Truss. Place them in a baking tin or shallow casserole. Grind a liberal amount of black pepper onto the skin of the poussins. Surround poussins with shallots. Put 6 mm/¼ inch of water in the bottom of the tin. Bake for 45 minutes. Baste the poussins, adding a little water to pan if necessary.

While the poussins are baking, peel the parsnips and cut them into 5-cm/2-inch pieces. Bring to a boil in salted water. Lower the heat and simmer 25 to 30 minutes, until very tender. Transfer them with a slotted spoon to a food processor or blender. Process until very smooth. Keep warm. You should have 375 ml/12 fl oz.

After the poussins have baked for 45 minutes, put them under the grill for 30 seconds to brown. Remove the poussins and caramelized shallots from the grill.

Spoon the parsnip purée onto the bottom of a serving platter. Cut poussins in half, discarding string, and place on top of purée along with the shallots.

Serves 4

One Duck, Two Dinners

I. Braised Duck Legs with Apples and Sauerkraut

If "poultry is to the cook what canvas is to the painter," as Brillat-Savarin said, then here's artistic proof: two completely different-tasting preparations, each with only three ingredients.

> **1 duckling, about 2.5 kg/5 lb**
>
> **500 g/1 lb packaged sauerkraut**
>
> **2 large Granny Smith apples, unpeeled**

Cut the duck into the following pieces: 2 breast halves (no bones); 2 legs (with thighs). Reserve.

Use the neck, back, wings and gizzards (do not use the liver) to make a stock: Put the pieces in a medium-size heavy pan with about 1 litre/32 fl oz water, or to cover. Add 1 teaspoon whole black peppercorns. Simmer for 2 hours with the cover askew, then strain through a fine sieve. Return the stock to the pan and reduce slowly to 500 ml/16 fl oz. Reserve the stock for use in both duck preparations.

Preheat the oven to 180°C/350°F/gas 4.

Cook the duck legs slowly, turning several times, in a large non-stick frying pan for 10 minutes. Pour off the fat and reserve. The duck skin should be browned.

Drain the sauerkraut. Dice one apple into 6-mm/¼-inch cubes, removing the seeds. Mix with the sauerkraut and put in the bottom of a shallow casserole. Add ⅓ teaspoon whole black peppercorns, ½ teaspoon coarse salt, and 125 ml/4 fl oz duck stock. Place the duck legs on top and bake 45 minutes. Pour 3 tablespoons duck fat over

Splash sauerkraut with white wine or gin before baking. Boil tiny white potatoes until almost done, then sauté in duck fat until crisp and serve with the duck.

GRAPENOTE

Chill a bottle of Alsatian sylvaner or gewürztraminer and enjoy the marriage of body and flavours. My husband likes this dish with an off-dry bubbly, some of which he reluctantly adds to the sauerkraut before baking.

the duck and sauerkraut. Bake 15 minutes longer.

Cut the remaining apple into 10 to 12 wedges, removing the seeds. Heat 1 tablespoon duck fat in a small nonstick frying pan and sauté the apples over high heat until browned and soft. Remove the casserole from the oven. Put the sauerkraut and the duck legs on a platter and top with the sautéed apple slices.

II. Sautéed Duck Breasts with Green Olives and Sweet Vermouth

2 duck breast halves, bones removed

60 ml/2 fl oz sweet vermouth

60 g/2 oz French Picholine or Spanish green olives

Make several slashes in the skin of the duck. Season with coarse salt and freshly ground black pepper. Refrigerate several hours.

Put the duck breasts, skin side down, in a cold, large nonstick frying pan and cook slowly over medium heat until the fat is rendered. Pour the fat off. Turn the duck over and cook 5 to 6 minutes longer.

Preheat the grill.

Add 60 ml/2 fl oz of the reserved duck stock, the vermouth, and the olives to the pan. Increase the heat and cook 2 to 3 minutes. Remove the duck to a shallow baking tin or heavy-gauge flan tin and place under the grill to crisp the skin.

Reduce the juices in the pan until thickened. Place the duck breasts on a platter and pour the sauce and olives over the duck.

I, II: Serves 2

ADD-ONS

Serve on a purée of very buttery Perfect Mashed Potatoes (page 217), seasoned judiciously with freshly ground white pepper.

GRAPENOTE

The fragrant, briary fruit of a California or Oregon pinot noir makes a compelling match. Soft tannins and good acidity do nice things for the duck.

Michael's Perfect Roast Turkey
with Lemon and Sage

My husband—food and restaurant consultant by day, intellectual smartass by night—devised this solution to the age-old dilemma of dry breast meat or undercooked leg meat. "Ignore the darned popup timer," he says. "It guarantees an overcooked bird. Invest instead in a good meat thermometer." This is a wordy but worthy recipe.

> 8- to 10-kg/16- to 18-lb fresh turkey, at room
> temperature
>
> 2 tablespoons dried sage leaves (see Note)
>
> 2 large lemons

Preheat the oven to 165°C/325°F/gas 3.

Remove the fat from the rear of the turkey. Melt it in a small non-stick frying pan. Set aside.

Starting at the neck of the turkey, slip your fingers under the skin and carefully separate the skin from one entire side of the breast; most of your hand eventually will be under the skin. Continue downwards and, with your index finger, separate the skin around the thigh. Repeat on the other side of the bird.

Crumble the sage leaves and sprinkle them with freshly ground black pepper. Spread 1 tablespoon of sage on breast and thigh, beneath the skin, on each half of the turkey. Prick each lemon several times and insert in the bird's cavity.

Put the neck and giblets in a baking tin; do not use liver. With a pastry brush, thoroughly coat the breast with the rendered fat, then sprinkle the entire bird with more pepper. Fold a double thickness of kitchen paper in half and cover the entire breast. Carefully pour cold

ADD-ONS

Add white wine to pan juices before reducing. Serve with Wild Rice and Bulgur Toss (page 203) and Cranberry Chutney (page 286).

GRAPENOTE

Your choice: From an oaky Washington State chardonnay, to French Beaujolais, elegant Oregon pinot noir, or vibrant California zinfandel.

water on the paper to thoroughly moisten them, then cover the breast area with a foil tent. Place the bird on a rack over the gizzards and put it in the oven.

Every 20 minutes, pull the turkey from the oven, remove the foil tent, and thoroughly moisten the paper towels with cold water. Some water will flow into the pan and into the turkey; it will become part of your pan juices.

After 2½ hours, check the turkey temperature with a meat thermometer; the thigh should be about 60°C/145°F and the breast 50°C/125°F. If they are not, continue to cook (cooking time will depend on the initial temperature and on the size of the bird).

If they are, remove the foil and the kitchen paper and return the turkey to the oven for about 45 minutes. The breast will brown and temperatures will be about 82°C/180°F in the thigh and about 68°C/155°F in the breast.

Take the turkey out of the oven and remove the lemons. Tip the liquid inside the turkey into the roasting tin and then transfer all the pan juices and brown bits to a saucepan. Let the turkey rest under the foil tent. Skim the fat from the saucepan. Add ½ tablespoon juice from one of roasted lemons and bring to a boil. You should have about 375 ml/12 fl oz of liquid; either add water or reduce the liquid accordingly. Carve the turkey and serve with the pan juices.

Serves 12 to 14

Note: Buy whole dried sage leaves from a Middle Eastern or spice shop Do not use powdered sage.

Roast Veal with Leeks and Rosé Wine

When you want a meal that is comforting but impressive, try this. A boned loin of veal or a rolled and tied boneless veal shoulder are cuts that are often ignored. Slow braising, on a bed of leeks and in vapours of rosé wine, yields a very tender roast with a delicate flavour.

> **1 kg/2 lb boned loin of veal, or boneless veal shoulder rolled and tied**
>
> **6 large leeks**
>
> **250 ml/8 fl oz dry French rosé wine.**

Preheat the oven to 180°C/350°F/ gas 4.

Rub salt and freshly ground black pepper into the surface of the veal.

Trim off the green part of the leeks and reserve. Slice the white part of the leeks lengthwise and wash carefully. Cut into 12-mm/½-inch slices. Put the leeks in the bottom of a large heavy casserole.

Sear the veal quickly on all sides in a nonstick pan. Place the veal on top of the leeks. Add 60 ml/2 fl oz water, bring to a boil, and scrape the pan with a wooden spoon. Pour the pan liquid and the wine into the casserole. Cover and cook 1 hour. Reduce the heat to 150°C/300°F/ gas 2 and cook 1¼ hours longer, or until very tender. Remove the meat. Let rest while you prepare the sauce. If desired, cut the green part of the leeks into diamond shapes and boil 2 to 3 minutes. Use as a garnish.

Purée half the leeks in a blender on low speed, adding enough pan juices to make a thick sauce. If necessary, add water. Process until very smooth. Pass the sauce through a coarse sieve. Add salt to taste. Slice the meat and serve it over a mound of the remaining leeks. Cover with sauce and garnish with diamond-shaped leeks.

Serves 4 to 6

ADD-ONS

Sprinkle the sauce with pink peppercorns. Serve with Perfect Mashed Potatoes (page 217).

GRAPENOTE

Serve with the same French (or Spanish) rosé that was used to cook the veal.

Osso Buco with Tomatoes and Black Olives

A riff on the traditional Milanese dish, my osso buco (literally "bone with a hole") is based on only three ingredients: shanks of milk-fed veal, canned tomatoes, and oil-cured olives. Another twist is the coupling of this fork-tender veal with saffron orzo (instead of traditional rice). What remains the same is the standard add-on of gremolata: grated lemon zest, garlic and parsley—another quick "1-2-3."

> 4 osso buco (veal hind knuckle cut into 5-cm/
> 2-inch-thick pieces, bone marrow in centre),
> about 1.5 kg/3 lb
>
> 1 (880-g/28-oz) can plum tomatoes in juice,
> 125 ml/4 fl oz reserved for another use
>
> 60 g/2 oz oil-cured black olives

In a large nonstick frying pan, brown the osso buco for 3 to 4 minutes on each side. Remove the meat, pour 125 ml/4 fl oz water into the pan, and boil until reduced to 60 ml/2 fl oz.

Place the browned meat in a heavy shallow casserole. Pour the pan liquid, the tomatoes and the juice over the top of the meat. Scatter the olives over the juices. Cover the casserole tightly and simmer over low heat for 1 hour. Uncover, turn the meat over, cover, and continue to cook for 45 to 50 minutes, until very tender. Remove the meat to a platter.

Reduce the sauce over high heat, breaking up the tomatoes a little with a wooden spoon. Cook until the juices thicken substantially, then add salt and pepper to taste. Pour over the osso buco and serve.

Serves 4

Grilled Veal Chop, Yellow Tomato Coulis, and Basil Oil

About a decade ago, scaloppine were displaced by grilled chops as the most trendy and desirable cut of veal. A satisfying dish that bridges the seasons, the veal chop is equally delicious with red tomato coulis when yellow ones are unavailable.

4 rib veal chops, each 3 cm/1¼ inches thick

Basil Oil (page 156), warmed

Yellow Tomato Coulis (page 156), warmed

Preheat the oven to 180°C/350°F/gas 4.

Season the veal chops with salt and freshly ground black pepper. Brush lightly with some of the basil oil.

In a well-seasoned cast-iron frying pan, sear the veal chops on both sides until browned. Finish cooking in the oven until done, about 15 minutes.

Divide the tomato coulis evenly on the plates. Top with the veal chops and spoon more basil oil over the top.

Serves 4

ADD-ONS

Garnish with fresh basil and Slow-Roasted Plum Tomatoes (page 220).

GRAPENOTE

A luscious red Italian wine with a touch of berry fruit makes a special partner for this dish. Try a Rosso di Montalcino. Want something French? Open a Rully Rouge, medium-bodied with a true Burgundian bouquet.

Yellow Tomato Coulis

375 g/12 oz large yellow tomatoes, blanched and peeled
1 tablespoon extra-virgin olive oil

Cut the tomatoes in half and squeeze out the seeds. Cut in large pieces. Place the tomatoes in a blender, add the oil, and purée until smooth. Add salt and pepper to taste.

Makes 180 ml/6 fl oz

Basil Oil

1 large bunch fresh basil
6 tablespoons extra-virgin olive oil

Remove the leaves from the stems and wash. Blanch the leaves in boiling water for 1 minute. Plunge in iced water. Drain and gently squeeze the water from the basil. Place in a blender. Add oil and purée until smooth. Add salt to taste. Refrigerate.

Makes 150 ml/5 fl oz

Arista: Roast Loin of Pork with Rosemary and Garlic

I was nineteen, in Siena, and in love with Italy when I tasted my first arista; nothing has erased the memory of this triumphant marriage of ingredients. Have it with a glass of Chianti, as I did. Kiss your butcher, and ask him to saw through the bones for easy carving.

1.75- to 2-kg/3½- to 4-lb loin of pork, bones trimmed but not removed

3 tablespoons fresh rosemary leaves, minced

2 tablespoons finely chopped fresh garlic

Pat the loin of pork dry with kitchen paper. In a pestle and mortar, or with a fork and wooden board, make a coarse paste of the rosemary, the garlic, ½ teaspoon salt and ½ teaspoon coarse ground black pepper. Spread all over the loin of pork and let stand for 1 hour.

Preheat the oven to 165°C/325°F/gas 3.

Roast for 1½ hours (about 25 minutes per 500g/1 lb) or until a meat thermometer reads 68°C/155°F. Let meat rest while making the sauce.

Add boiling water and 1 to 2 teaspoons freshly chopped rosemary leaves to the pan juices. Slice the pork and serve with the pan juices.

ADD-ONS

You can deglaze the pan with white wine, if desired. Serve with Broccoli di Rape with Anchovies and Pine Nuts (page 196). To serve cold: Slice thin and cover with a veil of Anchovy-Lemon Mayonnaise (page 139).

GRAPENOTES

Try a geographically correct Chianti Classico to accompany this fragrant pork roast.

Barbecued Pork Pull

This is a pungent, mouthwatering dish that triggers ISR (instant salivary response). It sticks not only to your ribs but also to your pan, so cook it in Teflon for easy cleaning. Serve with Cheddar-Pepper Grits (page 199) and let the good times roll.

1 pork shoulder roast, about 3 kg/6 lb

375 ml/12 fl oz cider vinegar

250 ml/8 fl oz ketchup

Preheat the oven to 180°C/300°F/gas 4.

Brown the pork in a large nonstick frying pan and then place it in a heavy casserole. Mix the cider vinegar, the ketchup, 500 ml/16 fl oz water, 2 teaspoons salt and lots of freshly ground black pepper in a saucepan and bring to a boil. Pour it over the pork and cover.

Bake 40 minutes to the 500 g/1 lb, basting occasionally with drippings. Turn once every hour. The meat should be very soft when done.

Transfer the pork to a chopping board. Remove the meat from the bone and chop it into fairly fine pieces. Add any solids from the cooking liquid to the meat. Season to taste with additional vinegar, salt and pepper.

Makes 1.1 kg/2¼ pounds, serving 6

ADD-ONS

Serve with your own "Condiment Bar": Put an assortment of hot sauces on a tray and pass to your guests. Serve with good-quality white bread or freshly made Beer Bread (page 101).

GRAPENOTE

Have a beer . . .
or two.

Pork Chops with Vinegar Peppers

Peperoncini, a sprightly Italian condiment of little green hot peppers in a vinegary brine, makes a mouthwatering foil for thick, meaty pork chops. Sauté the chops slowly for optimum moistness. This will surely become a family favourite.

> **250 g/8 oz peperoncini, drained**
>
> **4 thick pork chops, 155 to 185 g/5 to 6 oz each**
>
> **4½ tablespoons good-quality olive oil**

Drain the jar of peperoncini. Pick out the smallest peppers to use.

Dust the pork chops with salt and freshly ground black pepper. Heat 1 tablespoon of the olive oil in a large nonstick frying pan. Sauté the chops on each side until cooked to the desired degree of doneness, being careful not to overcook. Remove from the pan and keep warm.

Add 3½ tablespoons olive oil to the pan, scraping up any browned bits. Add the peppers and sauté for 3 to 4 minutes, until soft. Pour the peppers and the oil over the pork chops. Serve immediately.

Serves 4

ADD-ONS

Add 2 cloves of thinly sliced garlic to the pan with the peppers. Serve with hot, crusty Italian bread.

GRAPENOTE

Two different styles of wine will satisfy in very different ways. Try a bold chilled Lindemans Semillon-Chardonnay with a touch of sweetness to complement hot and spicy flavours. Or try an inky red wine equal to the considerable heft of the dish—such as Salice Salentino, from southern Italy.

Roast Pork Tenderloin
with Prunes and Bay Leaves

GRAPENOTE

A chardonnay or
Beaujolais, depending
on your choice of
accompaniments.

In France, where the mention of prunes never causes a chuckle, this dish would have a distinct bistro feel. Try with Winter Squash and Orange Purée (page 179) and a chardonnay. For a different style, have it with Caramelized Chicory and Bacon (page 176) and a glass of Beaujolais.

8 fresh bay leaves

15 large stoned prunes

750 g/1½ lb pork tenderloin

Place the bay leaves and prunes in a bowl. Pour 375 ml/12 fl oz boiling water over the top and let sit 15 minutes.

Preheat the oven to 200°C/400°F/gas 6.

Make a 2.5-cm/1-inch-deep slit along the length of the tenderloin, leaving 2.5 cm/1 inch uncut on each end.

Remove the bay leaves and prunes from the water and pat dry with kitchen paper. Place the prunes in the bottom of the slit in a tight row. Crumble 1 bay leaf finely and sprinkle it over the prunes.

Roll the meat and tie it tightly at 2.5-cm/1-inch intervals. Sprinkle with salt and pepper on all sides. Place the remaining bay leaves under the strings.

Spray a baking tin with vegetable-oil cooking spray and place the tenderloin in the tin. Roast for 30 to 35 minutes. Let rest 5 minutes before slicing. Remove the bay leaves.

Serves 4

Garlic Sausage, Lentils and Diced Carrots

French garlic sausage or Italian cotechino are required for this robust country dish—its ingredients belong to both countries. These styles of sausages are made with the fattier parts of the pig and need to be cooked. You can find some great garlic sausages or ask your Italian delicatessen for cotechino.

> 750 g/1½ lb garlic sausage or cotechino sausage
>
> 375 g/12 oz lentils
>
> 3 large carrots, peeled

Put the sausage in a large pan and cover with 2 litres/64 fl oz cold water. Bring to a boil, lower the heat, and simmer 45 minutes. Remove the sausage and set aside.

Wash the lentils, drain, and add to the sausage cooking liquid. Bring to a boil. Add ½ teaspoon whole black peppercorns, lower the heat, and cook the lentils 35 to 40 minutes, until they are soft but not falling apart. Drain and keep warm.

Meanwhile, dice the carrots into 3-mm/⅛-inch cubes. Boil in a small amount of salted water for 8 minutes, or until soft. Drain and keep warm.

When ready to serve, boil the sausage in water for 2 minutes to reheat. Place the warm lentils on a platter. Cut the sausage into 2.5-cm/1-inch-thick slices and place on top. Scatter the carrots over the sausage and lentils. Serve immediately.

Serves 4

A few leaves of fried sage would be nice, as would a small pot of Dijon mustard.

GRAPENOTES

French? Serve full-bodied Beaujolais. Italian? Drink Nebbiolo. New Year's Eve? Drink champagne.

Calf's Liver with Home-Dried Grapes

ADD-ONS

Add 2 tablespoons brandy to the pan juices and grapes. Cook 1 minute over high heat to let alcohol evaporate. Garnish with fresh chervil.

GRAPENOTE

Relish with a graceful California pinot noir or elegant French red Burgundy.

Not a liver lover? You won't be able to resist these rosy, thin slices of tender meat punctuated with bursts of sweet grape flavour. Grapes prepared in this manner are halfway down the road to raisins but are more voluptuous. Serve with Gratin Dauphinoise (page 192) for a memorable meal.

> **500 g/1 lb red and green seedless grapes (or just green seedless)**
>
> **500 g/1 lb calf's liver, in one piece**
>
> **30 g/1 oz unsalted butter**

Preheat the oven to 200°C/400°F/gas 6.

Place the grapes on a baking tray and roast for 25 minutes, shaking the pan several times during roasting to prevent sticking. Reduce the oven temperature to 135°C/275°F/gas 1. Bake for an additional 40 minutes. Remove from the oven and reserve.

Sprinkle the liver with salt and freshly ground black pepper. In a nonstick frying pan, melt 15 g/½ oz butter. When it starts to brown, add the liver and sauté on both sides until the liver begins to crisp on the outside but is still pinkish on the inside.

Add the reserved grapes and cook 1 or 2 minutes. Remove the liver to a warm platter, leaving the grapes in the pan. Add the remaining butter to the pan with a few tablespoons boiling water and heat sauce 1 minute over high heat, scraping any browned bits off the bottom of the pan. Slice the liver on the bias and pour the sauce over the top.

Serves 4

Lamb Shanks Alsatian-Style

Inspired by a dish at Restaurant JoJo, in New York, I created a version of Alsatian "baeckeofe," or "baker's oven," using my favourite hunk of meat: a lamb shank (hind knuckle). Make sure your enamel-glazed casserole has a secure cover, as you want the shanks to bathe in their winy onion sauce.

2 large lamb shanks, 750 g/1½ lb each

625 g/1¼ lb onions

500 ml/16 fl oz dry Alsatian riesling

Preheat the grill.

Salt and pepper the lamb shanks and place them on a baking tray. Grill 5 minutes on each side. Remove from the grill. Lower the heat to 180°C/350°F/gas 4. Peel the onions and slice them in half lengthwise, then across into 6-mm/¼-inch-thick slices. Put in the bottom of a heavy shallow casserole (an enamel Le Creuset is best).

Place the shanks on the onions. Cover and bake 1 hour. Turn shanks and add 375 ml/12 fl oz wine. Cover and bake 1 hour longer.

Remove the shanks with tongs to a warm platter. Place the casserole on top of the stove. Add 125 ml/4 fl oz white wine and salt and pepper to taste. Cook over medium-high heat, scraping up any browned bits, for 2 minutes to finish sauce. Pour over the lamb shanks.

Serves 2

ADD-ONS

Serve with French Potato Cake (page 207).

GRAPENOTE

Continue to drink the good-quality wine you used in cooking this dish, or go up the flavour scale a bit and serve Pinot Auxerrois, also from Alsace.

Lamb Steaks with Tomatoes and Za'atar

One bite will transport you to the land of the Pharaohs, where lamb is king of the meal. A sauce of za'atar and tomatoes lends an unfamiliar yet haunting flavour to a juicy lamb steak cut from the leg. You can substitute shoulder chops, but they won't be as tender.

1 (880-g/28-oz) can plum tomatoes in juice

2 tablespoons za'atar spice

6 lamb steaks or shoulder chops,
250 g/8 oz each

Put the tomatoes and juice in a medium-size heavy pan and cook slowly over low heat for 20 minutes, mashing lightly with a spoon or potato masher. Add za'atar and cook 10 minutes longer; the sauce will become thick. Reserve. Makes 500 ml/16 fl oz.

Season the lamb with salt and freshly ground pepper. In a large nonstick frying pan, sear the lamb on both sides until crisp and rare. Add the sauce and heat 5 minutes.

Serves 6

ADD-ONS

Add crumbled feta cheese to the top of the sauce and bake in the oven at 200°C/400°F/gas 6 for 2 to 3 minutes. Serve with basmati rice.

GRAPENOTE

Now's the time for a blockbuster merlot from California. Or a merlot from Yarden Winery in Israel's Golan Heights or a Château Musar red wine from Lebanon.

Rack of Lamb with Pesto Crumbs

Definitely a dish for a VIP. Choose a rack from a young lamb and ask your butcher to prepare the ends of the bones by scraping them clean just up to the eye of the meat. You can use a good-quality prepared pesto, or if you can handle a few more ingredients, make your own. Fresh bread crumbs are a must. Honour your guest with a glass of mouth-filling Côtes Rôtie or Shiraz from Australia.

> **750-g/1½-lb rack of lamb, trimmed, flap removed, bones exposed (8 ribs)**
>
> **80 ml/3 fl oz pesto sauce—plus more for serving if desired**
>
> **60 g/2 oz breadcrumbs made from fresh bread**

Preheat the oven to 190°C/375°F/gas 5.

Season the lamb with salt and freshly ground black pepper. Spread the pesto sauce over the surface of the meat.

Coat the meat thoroughly with bread crumbs. Cover the bones with foil and place the lamb on a baking tray. Roast for 15 minutes, remove the foil, and bake 20 minutes longer. Remove from the oven, let rest 5 minutes, and carve, slicing into thick double chops or single chops. Serve with additional pesto sauce if desired.

Serves 2 to 4

GRAPENOTE

Spend some money for a great Côtes Rôtie, such as Domaine de Bonserine from France; or drink Penfolds Bin 389 cabernet-shiraz from Australia.

Turkish Lamb Chops

Worthy of a sultan, this authentic preparation of thick loin chops typifies the sensational grilled meats of the eastern Mediterranean. If an outdoor barbecue is not handy, sear in a cast-iron grill pan or grill close to the source of heat. Nice with a squeeze of fresh lemon and a helping of Turkish Pilaf with Tomato.

2 large onions, grated

80 ml/3 fl oz extra-virgin olive oil

12 loin lamb chops, 2.5-cm/1-inch thick

Sprinkle the grated onions with 1 teaspoon salt. Squeeze out the juice of the onions and discard. Mix the onions with the oil. Brush the lamb chops on both sides with this marinade, and let stand for 1 hour.

Barbecue the chops, preferably over charcoal, on both sides. Sprinkle with salt and lots of cracked black pepper.

Serves 4

ADD-ONS

Place 2 tablespoons fresh thyme leaves in the marinade. Serve the lamb chops with wedges of fresh lemon, fried potatoes, or authentic Turkish Pilaf with Tomato (page 180).

GRAPENOTE

Serve with a robust merlot or a white with strong character, such as Greco di Tufo, from southern Italy, or even a white retsina from Greece.

Maple-Glazed Beef Brisket

A blustery March day, when the sap of mighty maples has started to rise, seems a good time to make this dish and celebrate St. Patrick's Day in an American fashion. Only the aromatic flavour of real maple syrup will do.

2 to 2.5 kg/4 to 5 lb beef brisket

30 whole cloves

125 ml/4 fl oz pure maple syrup

In an enamelled casserole, cover the beef with water and bring to a boil. Lower the heat, cover, and simmer until done, allowing 50 to 55 minutes per 500 g/1 lb. Place on a rack in an open roasting tin. Stick with whole cloves in a cross-hatch design.

Preheat the oven to 190°C/375°F/gas 5.

Pour the syrup over the meat and put in the oven to brown and glaze for about 15 minutes. Baste occasionally with syrup.

Serves 6 to 8

ADD-ONS

Serve with Chardonnay Cabbage (page 198) and boiled small new potatoes.

GRAPENOTE

You need a wine with a bit of sweetness: a chenin blanc or a rosé.

Coffee and Vinegar Pot Roast

I've collected over the years a stack of wacky and wonderful recipes from a variety of odd sources. Many come from community cooks, who are never shy about displaying naiveté. My favourite, originally known as Lutheran Ladies Peking Beef Roast, says to "burn on both sides and douse with coffee." Improbable perhaps, but delicious.

> **2.5-kg/5-lb beef chuck roast**
>
> **250 ml/8 fl oz white wine vinegar**
>
> **500 ml/16 fl oz strong, hot black coffee**

Put the meat in a large, nonmetallic bowl and pour the vinegar over it. Refrigerate 24 to 48 hours, turning several times.

Remove the meat from the marinade, reserving the vinegar. Pat the meat dry with kitchen paper and brown it in a heavy pan until nearly burned on both sides. The meat will generate its own fat.

Pour the coffee and 250 ml/8 fl oz water over the beef and scrape up the browned bits with a wooden spoon. Add 2 tablespoons whole black peppercorns (or a combination of both black and white) and ½ tablespoon salt. Cover and cook slowly for 3½ hours, or until fork-tender. Turn several times during cooking. Remove the meat and keep warm.

Add the reserved vinegar if desired, add salt and pepper to taste, and reduce the liquid until you have 750 ml/24 fl oz. Thinly slice the meat and heat in the gravy for ½ hour longer over very low heat.

Serves 6 to 8

ADD-ONS

Add 2 bay leaves to the cooking liquid. Serve with Turnip and Havarti Torte (page 177), Potato-Fennel Mash (page 190), or French Potato Cake (page 207).

GRAPENOTE

Try any one of the younger "cabs" from the New World or experiment with one of the new Meritage blends of cabernet, merlot, and cabernet franc.

Steak Haché, Cabernet Butter

Pretty fancy name for a hamburger, but this "chopped steak" does taste fancy under a blanket of buttery red wine sauce known as "beurre rouge." Serve with the veg du jour: Whole Roasted Garlic with Goat Cheese (page 184). Go ahead and finish that bottle of cabernet.

625 g/1¼ lb finely chopped beef sirloin

45 g/1½ oz unsalted butter, cold

125 ml/4 fl oz cabernet sauvignon

Divide the beef into two equal portions. Mould into large oval shapes, to look something like a steak. Season with salt and freshly ground black pepper.

In a large nonstick frying pan, melt 7 g/¼ oz of the butter. Add the meat and sear on each side 3 to 4 minutes, so that the outside is well browned and the inside is rare to medium-rare.

Remove the "steaks" to platter. Add the wine to the pan and reduce over high heat. Add ½ teaspoon coarse ground black pepper and salt to taste. When reduced by half, remove from the heat and whisk in the remaining cold butter. Pour the sauce over the "steaks." Serve immediately.

Serves 2

Add 1 tablespoon drained green pepper-corns to the sauce instead of black pepper.

GRAPENOTE

Open a bottle of your favourite cabernet sauvignon, a not-too-expensive Bordeaux, or a Spanish red Rioja.

Pan-Seared Sirloin, Oyster Sauce Reduction

ADD-ONS

Garnish with fresh chopped chives. To serve Carpetbag-style, top with plump poached oysters.

GRAPENOTE

White wine with meat? Try a blockbuster barrel-fermented chardonnay from California or Australia. If you believe in red, try a bodacious Cornas or Amarone.

If there were such a thing as a Chinese steakhouse, this is the sort of dish it would serve—strong in flavour and suave in texture. As a twist on a classic called Carpetbag Steak, which is steak and oysters, top with several of the plump juicy bivalves, poached briefly in simmering water.

4 rump steaks, 375 g/12 oz each

50 g/1¾ oz unsalted butter, cold

3 tablespoons Chinese oyster sauce

On a clean tea towel, crack 4 teaspoons white peppercorns with a hammer or the flat side of a cleaver. Press the cracked peppercorns into the top of each steak, pounding lightly with your fist.

Melt 7 g/¼ oz of the butter in a large nonstick frying pan. Cook the steaks over high heat on each side until lightly caramelized. Remove the steaks and keep warm.

Add the oyster sauce to the pan. Bring to a boil. Remove from the heat and whisk in the remaining butter, cut into small pieces. The sauce will get creamy.

Slice the steaks thickly on the bias, or leave whole. Pour the sauce over the top.

Serves 4

Mahogany Short Ribs

This irreverent merger of foodstuffs results in a tantalizing dish that will amaze and amuse your guests. Prune juice tenderizes marbled ribs of beef, while teriyaki sauce adds a touch of sweetness and salinity. Nice with a bright, young zinfandel.

> **1.5 kg/3 lb rolled rib joint, cut into 4 pieces (see Note)**
>
> **250 ml/ 8 fl oz teriyaki sauce**
>
> **250 ml/8 fl oz prune juice**

Cover the meat in a mixture of teriyaki sauce and prune juice. Refrigerate, covered, overnight.

Remove the ribs from the marinade. Bring the marinade to a boil in a large pan with 250 ml/ 8 fl oz water and ½ teaspoon whole black peppercorns. Lower the heat, add the meat, and cover. Simmer for 2 hours, or until meat is very tender.

Remove the ribs to a platter. Reduce the sauce for 5 minutes or until syrupy over medium-high heat. Pour it over ribs.

This is also delicious the next day. Remove any congealed fat from the top of the sauce and slowly reheat the ribs in the liquid.

Serves 4

Note: Ask the butcher to cut the joint between the ribs into 4 pieces. Trim off the outer flap.

ADD-ONS

Serve with freshly cooked broad Egg Noodles with Butter and Rosemary (page 214). Top with a mound of steamed haricots verts for drama.

GRAPENOTE

Uncork a bottle of California zinfandel and let it "open" in the glass before serving the main course. Its rich berry taste and long finish will balance the sweetness and salinity in this dish. Look for zins that are labelled "old vines" for the most concentrated fruit.

Fillet of Beef,
Gorgonzola Whipped Potatoes

ADD-ONS

Serve with Melted
Tomatoes (page 221)
or French Beans with
Toasted Hazelnuts
(page 182)

GRAPENOTE

Lots of wonderful
possibilities: try
Chateau Gloria; a
warm lusty red from
the Côtes du Rous-
sillon; a Spanish
Tempranillo from
Ribera del Duero, or a
California cab from
Mondavi.

This sounds like a he-man recipe, but the result is really a sophisticated dish for entertaining. The meat is at its best when rare. Serve with a special-occasion cabernet or French Bordeaux.

750 g/1½ lb potatoes

185 g/6 oz Italian Gorgonzola or Cambazola cheese

1.25 kg/2½ lb fillet of beef

Peel the potatoes and cut into quarters. Place in a pan with salted water to cover. Bring to a boil, lower heat, and simmer 30 to 40 minutes, until soft. Transfer the potatoes to the bowl of electric mixer. Reserve 125 ml/4 fl oz of the cooking liquid. Cut the cheese into small pieces and add it to the potatoes. Whip until light and fluffy. Add a little cooking liquid if necessary. Add salt and pepper.

Preheat the oven to 200°C/400°F/gas 6.

Season the fillet with salt and pepper. Put on a baking tray and roast 25 to 30 minutes, until the meat reaches an internal temperature of 54°C/130°F. Remove from oven and let rest 10 minutes.

Warm the potatoes in a heavy pan over low heat, stirring often. Spoon the potatoes into the centre of 6 large, warm dinner plates. Carve the fillet into 4-cm/1½-inch-thick slices. Put a slice on top of each mound of potatoes. Spoon any pan juices over the meat.

Serves 6

Hot Tip: To make mashed potato soup, add 250 ml/8 fl oz potato cooking liquid to potato-cheese mixture. Bring to boil. Pass through coarse sieve. Serve hot. Makes 625 ml/1 pint.

Prime Ribs of Beef, Horseradish-Rye Crust

As families have become smaller, we've forgotten the domestic pleasure of roast prime ribs of beef. The twist here lies in the pungency of horseradish that is punched up by the flavour of caraway.

> **3 to 3.5 kg/6 to 7 lb standing ribs of beef, tied (3 or 4 ribs), at room temperature**
>
> **6 tablespoons prepared white horseradish**
>
> **8 slices rye bread with caraway seeds, made into breadcrumbs**

Preheat oven to 150°C/300°F/gas 2.

Place the meat on a rack in a roasting tin and put it in the oven. Remove roast from oven after 90 minutes. Increase the oven temperature to 200°C/400°F/gas 6. Carefully drain any fat and juices from the tin and reserve. Coat the exterior of the roast with horseradish. Cover evenly with breadcrumbs, packing it down with your hands. Sprinkle with salt and freshly ground black pepper. Drizzle the pan juices over the crumbs.

Return the roast to the oven. Finish cooking until desired doneness is reached, about 30 minutes. A meat thermometer should read about 60°C/140°F for rare, 66°C/150°F for medium rare.

Serves 6 to 8

ADD-ONS

Serve with Turnip and Havarti Torte (page 177) and Sugar Snaps in Orange Butter (page 191).

GRAPENOTE

Try a bottle of voluptuous Bonny Doon Syrah; Cahors from the Dordogne, or the Hungarian Egri Bikaver, affectionately known as "bull's blood."

Chapter 10

Vegetables and Side Dishes

●

Sexy and inexpensive, side dishes are stealing the show in all the best restaurants. Why not at home?

Today the accent is on intriguing and unexpected starches—the mashed potato has been elevated to celebrity status—and vegetable accompaniments are designed to knock your socks off.

Bulgur and barley, couscous and polenta, grits and rice, even the humble bean carry flavours easily and have a comforting feel in the mouth. They mould into interesting shapes and are delicious at a variety of temperatures.

Best of all, my three-ingredient vegetables and side dishes have high flavour profiles and assertive textures; in combination, they constitute terrific meatless meals.

Caramelized Chicory and Bacon

The torpedoes of slender white leaves that we know as chicory are usually used in salad. But this braised dish—a fascinating balance of bitter, sweet, salt and smoke—is handsome enough to serve by itself as a first course or an indulgent side dish.

4 medium or large heads chicory

8 slices bacon

2 tablespoons balsamic vinegar

Preheat the oven to 200°C/400°F/gas 6.

Remove any dark or bruised outer leaves. Wrap 2 slices of bacon around each chicory in a spiral and secure with wooden cocktail sticks. Place the chicory in a shallow baking dish with 60 ml/2 fl oz water. Bake for 40 minutes. Sprinkle each chicory with ½ tablespoon vinegar, turn, and bake 10 minutes longer.

Remove from the oven. Sprinkle with additional balsamic vinegar and freshly ground black pepper. Serve hot as a side dish or at room temperature as a first course.

Serves 4

Turnip and Havarti Torte

*My simplified adaptation of a medieval recipe turns a much-reviled root
vegetable into a refined accompaniment that looks surprisingly like a
cake. It's a delicious foil for full-flavoured or fatty meats like duck and
pork—I even love it cold. Use large white turnips for the prettiest results.*

> **1.25 kg/2½ lb large white turnips**
>
> **30 g/1 oz unsalted butter, at room temperature**
>
> **500 g/1 lb caraway havarti cheese, in 2-mm/
> ¹⁄₁₆-inch slices**

Boil the unpeeled turnips in salted water for 30 minutes or until
tender. Drain, cool, peel, and cut into 6-mm/¼-inch-thick slices. Pat
dry with kitchen paper.

Preheat the oven to 190°C/375°F/gas 5.

Spread the butter in the bottom of a 23-cm/9-inch springform tin.
Arrange layer of cheese on bottom, using a quarter of the cheese.
Add a layer of turnip slices (overlapping slightly) and sprinkle very
lightly with salt and freshly ground pepper. Continue layering (another two layers), ending with a layer of cheese on top. Place the tin
on a baking tray.

Bake 40 minutes. When finished, the cheese should be golden
brown. Let cool slightly before serving. Remove from the tin. Cut
into wedges.

This is even better the next day when reheated.

Serves 10 to 12

Fried Lemon and Courgette Salad

This may be my favourite edible invention. A wake-up call to your taste buds, this dish adds syncopated bursts of Mediterranean flavour to fish, veal and lamb. If there's any left over, try it instead of mundane tomato in a sandwich.

500 g/1 lb medium courgettes

Olive oil, about 80 ml/3 fl oz

2 large thin-skinned lemons

Wash the courgettes. Slice on a bias, about 8 mm/⅓ inch thick. Sprinkle with 1 teaspoon salt and place in colander. Let stand 1 hour. Rinse well and dry thoroughly.

In a medium-size frying pan, fry small batches quickly in hot shallow oil, turning once, until golden brown. Drain on kitchen paper and place in a bowl.

Slice the lemons very thin. Add to the hot oil and fry, turning once. The lemons will brown and the oil will thicken into a delicious sauce. Add the cooked lemons to the courgettes and add some of the lemon oil. Let marinate one hour at room temperature before serving. Sprinkle with salt and freshly ground black pepper.

Serves 4

ADD-ONS

You can add 1 teaspoon freshly minced garlic to the bowl while marinating, or 1 tablespoon finely chopped mint.

COOK'S TIP

Serve with freshly grilled or steamed halibut or red snapper. Also delicious alongside grilled lamb kebabs.

Winter Squash and Orange Purée

Forget all those watery squashes that ruined Aunt Maud's dinners! This is an intense, perfumed recipe that adds great interest (and a brilliant orange colour) to simple roast birds and meats. You can use most winter squash, like butternut, acorn or pumpkin.

1 kg/2 lb winter squash

1 orange

30 g/1 oz unsalted butter

Preheat the oven to 200°C/400°F/gas 6.

Cut the squash in half lengthwise, then in half crosswise. Remove seeds and any membrane. Place in baking tin flesh side down and pour 60 ml/2 fl oz water over the top. Bake for 1 hour, turning over after 30 minutes. Squash will be lightly caramelized.

Remove the flesh from the skin, put it in a food processor and purée until smooth. Add 2 teaspoons freshly grated orange zest and 2 tablespoons fresh orange juice. Cut the butter into small pieces and add it to the processor. Process again. Add salt and pepper to taste.

Makes 500 ml/16 fl oz, serving 4 to 5

Turkish Pilaf with Tomato

"Handkerchief steaming" is what makes this dish authentically Turkish. It is a great pilaf, the texture tantamount to perfection.

250 ml/8 oz long-grain rice or basmati rice

15 g/½ oz unsalted butter

500 ml/16 fl oz tomato juice

Place the rice in a bowl with 2 teaspoons salt. Pour boiling water over, stir, and let stand until water cools. Drain the rice, wash it well under cold water and drain again. Set aside.

Place the butter, the tomato juice and 1 teaspoon salt in a heavy saucepan and bring to a boil. Add the rice, stir, cover, and boil over high heat for 2 minutes. Lower heat and cook slowly until the rice absorbs all the liquid.

Turn off the heat, uncover, place a clean handkerchief or tea towel over the saucepan, replace the cover and let the pilaf stand for 30 minutes before serving. A wooden spoon is recommended to transfer pilaf from saucepan to serving plate.

Serves 4

Put a small cinnamon stick in the water when boiling the rice. Remove before serving.

Watercress Purée
("Tastes Like Creamed Spinach")

Small, peppery watercress is overlooked as a vegetable. When cooked, it makes an AstroTurf-green purée that will rival the best creamed spinach. Spoon into a large, hot baked potato for a great supper.

> 375 g/12 oz boiling potatoes
>
> 500 g/1 lb watercress (4 large bunches),
>   washed well
>
> 45 g/1½ oz unsalted butter, cold, cut into
>   several pieces

Bring 2 litres/64 fl oz of water plus 1½ teaspoons salt to a boil. Peel potatoes. Slice in half lengthwise, then across into 12-mm/½-inch slices. Place in boiling water, lower heat to medium, and cook 20 minutes.

Trim 4 cm/1½ inches off the stems of the watercress and discard. Add the watercress to the potatoes after 20 minutes and cook 10 minutes longer.

Drain. Transfer potatoes and watercress to food processor. Purée until thick and smooth, slowly adding the cold butter. Return to the heat and warm before serving. Add salt to taste (don't add pepper).

Makes 500 ml/16 fl oz, serving 4 to 5

ADD-ONS

A little freshly grated nutmeg brings out the flavour.

French Beans with Toasted Hazelnuts

ADD-ONS

Sprinkle the beans
with 1 teaspoon
tarragon vinegar while
sautéing.

Years ago, if you had a pile of thin, tiny green beans on your plate, you were either in Paris or in a French restaurant. Luckily, haricots verts are available today in many supermarkets and are particularly glamorous when tossed with bits of toasted hazelnuts.

> **500 g/1 lb haricots verts, trimmed (or green beans trimmed and julienned lengthwise)**
>
> **45 g/1½ oz coarsely chopped hazelnuts, lightly toasted**
>
> **45 g/1½ oz unsalted butter**

Bring salted water to a boil. Add the beans and blanch 5 minutes. Quickly shock in a colander under cold water. Drain well.

Just before serving, sauté the hazelnuts in the butter. Add the beans and, tossing lightly, heat until they are warm. Add salt and pepper to taste.

Serves 4 to 6

Courgette, Black Olive
and Tomato Compote

Move over, ratatouille; this triptych of Mediterranean flavours is as memorable, and much easier to prepare. A wonderful, jam-like accompaniment to grilled tuna or juicy medallions of veal, it is also great on a baguette with sliced hard-boiled eggs.

250 g/8 oz crushed tomatoes in juice

375 g/12 oz small courgettes

18 oil-cured black olives, stoned

In a large nonstick frying pan, heat the crushed tomatoes for 5 minutes over medium heat until slightly reduced.

Wash the courgettes and pat dry. Slice into 12-mm/½-inch-thick circles. Add to the tomatoes and cook for 15 to 20 minutes, or until the courgettes become soft and translucent. Add a few tablespoons of water if sauce is too thick. Add olives, ¼ teaspoon salt and lots of freshly ground black pepper. Continue to cook 2 to 3 minutes.

Let cool and serve at room temperature.

Makes 500 ml/16 fl oz, serving 4

ADD-ONS

Drizzle with a flavoured olive oil. Add several strips of fresh orange zest to tomatoes.

Whole Roast Garlic with Goat Cheese

ADD-ONS

Serve with mixed greens tossed with Lemon Vinaigrette (page 56) as a memorable salad course for company.

However unthinkable it may be to eat a head of garlic, this is so delicious it would be more unthinkable not to. The pulp becomes soft and spreadable and transfixingly mild. Serve with a crusty baguette.

4 whole large heads garlic

60 ml/2 fl oz aromatic olive oil

60 g/2 oz fresh goat cheese in a log

Preheat the oven to 150°C/300°F/gas 2.

Cut 8 mm/⅓ inch off the top of the heads of garlic. Put the garlic in a small baking dish with 3 tablespoons water. Sprinkle with 1 teaspoon coarse salt and drizzle oil over the tops of the garlic.

Bake, basting often, for 1¼ hours, or until the garlic cloves are very soft (many restaurants that serve this dish do not bake the garlic long enough).

Top each head with 15-g/½-ounce slice of goat cheese and grill 1 minute, or until golden.

Serves 4

Rosemary-Roast Potatoes

Cut in large wedges or homey chunks, these potatoes are designed to please. Long baking gives them an appealing crust enveloping a creamy interior. And rosemary is a potato's best friend.

8 medium potatoes (about 1 kg/2 lb)

3½ tablespoons chopped fresh rosemary (see Note)

60 ml/2 fl oz extra-virgin olive oil

Preheat the oven to 200°C/400°F/gas 6.

Peel the potatoes and cut them into 4 to 6 chunks or long wedges.

In a large bowl, make a paste of 3 tablespoons of the rosemary, the olive oil and 1½ teaspoons coarse salt. Add the potatoes and evenly coat them with the mixture, adding a little more oil if needed.

Place in a baking dish and bake 40 to 45 minutes, until browned, turning occasionally with a spatula.

Sprinkle with ½ tablespoon coarsely chopped fresh rosemary and additional coarse salt.

Serves 4 to 6

ADD-ONS

Add ½ teaspoon finely chopped garlic to rosemary-and-olive-oil mixture.

Note: You can substitute 2 teaspoons crumbled dried rosemary.

Smothered Lettuce with Sumac

You hardly ever come across cooked lettuce, but when gently sautéed with salty-sour sumac, iceberg yields its moisture and softens gracefully. This is a beguiling accompaniment to chicken and lamb, and even your foodie friends won't guess what it is.

ADD-ONS

Serve at room temperature with hot Med-Rim Lamb Nuggets (page 45), or as an unusual first course.

500 g/1 lb iceberg lettuce

3 tablespoons extra-virgin olive oil

1 tablespoon ground sumac (see Note)

Wash the lettuce, coarsely chop it and put it in a bowl with the olive oil. Mix well. Add sumac and toss.

Heat a large nonstick frying pan and put the lettuce mixture in the hot pan. Cook over medium-high heat 10 minutes, or until lettuce is wilted and dark green in colour. Drizzle with extra olive oil if desired. Add a pinch of salt and pepper. Serve hot or cold.

Serves 3 to 4

Note: Sumac is the small red berries of a shrub originating in Turkey, dried and ground into a powder that has a lemony, salty taste. Available in Middle Eastern food shops.

Steamed Broccoli, Stir-Fried Pecans

It's hard to believe that three simple ingredients can pack such a flavour wallop. This is one time you don't want your broccoli al dente but slightly soft to contrast better with the crunch of pecans. Definitely a crowd-pleasing, East-meets-West veggie.

1 large bunch broccoli

45 g/1½ oz coarsely chopped pecans

2 tablespoons Chinese oyster sauce

Cut the broccoli into large florets, leaving 4 cm/1½ inches of stem. You should have 500 g/1 lb florets (save the rest of the stems for another use). Steam the broccoli florets over boiling water for 8 to 10 minutes. They should be starting to soften but should still be bright green.

Meanwhile, toast the pecans in a nonstick frying pan until they become dark brown, being careful not to let them burn.

In a large bowl, toss the hot steamed broccoli, the toasted pecans, and the oyster sauce. Season to taste with sea salt and freshly ground black pepper. Serve immediately.

Serves 4

Spoonbread Custard

A "fallen soufflé" with a dense, creamy centre, this dish speaks of elegant Southern American hospitality. Serve it hot with cold buttermilk poured on top and pass the pepper mill. Or serve alongside Wild Greens and Blood Orange Salad (page 75) for a lovely lunch.

125 g/4 oz yellow cornmeal (polenta)

4 extra-large eggs, separated

250 ml/8 fl oz buttermilk

Preheat the oven to 200°C/400°F/gas 6.

Put the cornmeal in a bowl and add 250 ml/8 fl oz cold water. Put another 250 ml/8 fl oz of water in a saucepan with 1 teaspoon salt and bring to a boil. Stir in the wet cornmeal and cook 1 minute, stirring constantly with a wooden spoon. Remove from the heat. Add egg yolks, buttermilk, and freshly ground black pepper and mix well.

Beat the egg whites with a pinch of salt until thick. Fold into the cornmeal mixture.

Lightly coat a casserole with vegetable spray and pour the cornmeal mixture into the casserole. Bake 35 to 40 minutes, until golden brown and puffy. Serve hot with additional cold buttermilk poured on top.

Serves 6 to 8

White Polenta with Parmigiano-Reggiano

Polenta is usually made by adding cornmeal in a slow, steady stream to a pan of boiling water. Instead, when preparing white polenta, I add cold water to the cornmeal as a better way of reducing lumps. The result: white-on-white, ultra-creamy richness.

185 g/6 oz white cornmeal (polenta)

1 small clove garlic, pushed through a garlic press

7 tablespoons grated Parmigiano-Reggiano cheese

Place the white cornmeal and 1 teaspoon salt in a large saucepan. Gradually add 1.25 litres/2 pints water and then the garlic, stirring constantly with a wooden spoon to remove any lumps. Bring to a boil, reduce the heat to medium, and cook, uncovered, about 10 minutes. Add 5 tablespoons grated cheese and continue cooking and stirring frequently for 5 minutes more.

Spread the polenta on a heatproof platter, sprinkle with the remaining cheese, and grill 1 minute.

Serves 6 to 8

ADD-ONS

This is an interesting side dish when 125 g/ 4 oz cooked tiny frozen peas (petits pois) are added. As a first course, top with Grilled Shiitake Mushrooms, Garlic Essence (page 76). For "matzoh polenta," substitute matzoh meal for cornmeal.

Potato-Fennel Mash

An old-fashioned potato ricer is what gives this potato dish its special consistency. Fennel gives it a special taste. Decorate with feathery fennel fronds.

ADD-ONS

If you want a creamier consistency, add more butter or 2 or 3 table-spoons double cream.

750 g/1½ lb potatoes

375 g/12 oz fennel bulb, with fronds

45 g/1½ oz unsalted butter

Bring 1 litre/32 fl oz of water plus 1 teaspoon salt to a boil in large heavy pan. Peel potatoes and cut them into 12-mm/½-inch pieces. Cut the fronds off the fennel bulb and chop. Reserve. Trim any brown spots from the fennel and cut bulb into 12-mm/½-inch pieces. Put potatoes and fennel in boiling water.

Cook over medium heat for 40 minutes, or until very soft. Pass the potatoes and fennel through a potato ricer and return them to the pan to keep warm. Or transfer with a slotted spoon to a food processor and purée.

Add the butter and salt and freshly ground black pepper to taste. Mix in chopped fennel fronds.

Serves 6

Sugar Snaps in Orange Butter

A cross between garden peas and mangetout, sugar snap peas deliver what they promise: a sweet taste combined with a resonant crispness. Fresh orange juice adds perfume and emulsifies the butter into a delectable sauce.

500 g/1 lb sugar snap peas (see Note)

1 large orange

30 g/1 oz unsalted butter, cold

Trim the ends of the snap peas and remove the strings running down the length of the pods.

Bring a medium-size pan of salted water to a boil. Add the sugar snaps and cook 3 minutes, or until tender but not too soft. Their colour should remain a brilliant green.

Meanwhile, grate the orange zest on the medium-size holes of a hand grater. Reserve. Cut the orange in half.

When the sugar snaps are done, drain well in a colander and put them back in the pan. Add the orange zest, juice of ½ orange and the cold butter cut into small pieces. Heat slowly for 1 to 2 minutes until hot. Toss well. Add salt and pepper to taste. Serve warm.

Serves 4 to 6

Add-Ons

Scatter 1 teaspoon of black sesame seeds on top for a striking colour contrast.

Note: You can substitute mangetout.

Gratin Dauphinoise

A gratin is the golden, epicurean crust that forms on the surface of savoury baked or grilled dishes. Pungent Gruyère cheese makes a genial topping that acts as a protective layer, preventing the potatoes from drying out.

The classic potato Dauphinoise (from the Dauphiné in France) is made with cream, but there's some debate about the cheese.

1.25 kg/2½ lb potatoes

750 ml/24 fl oz single cream

125 g/4 oz grated Gruyère cheese

Peel the potatoes with a vegetable peeler, making sure to remove any black spots. Slice potatoes paper-thin with a sharp knife and put them in a pan, along with the cream, 2 teaspoons salt and some freshly ground white pepper. Stir well and simmer the potatoes in the cream for 15 minutes, or until potatoes are just beginning to soften.

Preheat the oven to 180°C/350°F/gas 4.

Transfer the potatoes and cream to a medium-size shallow casserole. The liquid should come just to the tops of the potatoes. Cover evenly with the grated cheese.

Bake 35 to 40 minutes, until potatoes are tender and cheese is golden brown.

Serves 6 to 8

Dry-Curry Sweet Potatoes

My sister-in-law invented an intriguing preparation for this autumnal vegetable that we usually heap sweet things upon. Instead, she gives sweet potatoes a curry rub, which transforms them into savoury, golden nuggets. Bet you can't eat just one.

750 g/1½ lb medium-to-large sweet potatoes

2 tablespoons good-quality curry powder

2 tablespoons olive oil

Preheat the oven to 200°C/400°F/gas 6.

Peel the sweet potatoes, using a vegetable peeler, and cut them into 2.5-cm/1-inch chunks. Place them in a medium-size, shallow casserole, sprinkle with the curry powder and 1 teaspoon salt and then drizzle olive oil evenly over the top.

Bake the potatoes for 45 minutes, turning them once or twice so they brown evenly and don't stick. Serve immediately.

Serves 4

Barley-Buttermilk Salad

ADD-ONS

Serve hot as a side dish drizzled with melted butter.

Barley is one of the oldest grains, going back to prehistoric times. Pearl barley—which has had the bran removed—absorbs flavours beautifully and is still extremely nutritious. Tossed with buttermilk dressing, it makes a tangy salad. Or serve it warm as an edible bed for Yogurt Chicken with Blackened Onions (page 145).

155 g/5 oz uncooked pearl barley

125 ml/4 fl oz buttermilk

3 tablespoons chopped fresh coriander

In a small enamel saucepan, bring 560 ml/18 fl oz water and 1 teaspoon salt to a boil. Add the barley, lower the heat and simmer 40 to 45 minutes, covered.

Drain well and put in a bowl. Add the buttermilk, the coriander and salt and pepper to taste. Mix well. Serve warm, at room temperature, or chilled. If barley becomes dry, add a little more buttermilk.

Serves 4 to 5

Bay-Smoked Potatoes

Use extra-fragrant bay leaves and your house will be enveloped in Mediterranean warmth. Not only does this exceptional method of "smoking" add perfume, it also blesses the potatoes with a creamy interior. They look beautiful on a platter, glistening with oil under a garland of these dark-green leaves of the laurel family.

> **1 kg/2 lb small-to-medium potatoes (about 8 to 10)**
>
> **14 bay leaves**
>
> **5 tablespoons extra-virgin olive oil**

Preheat the oven to 200°C/400°F/gas 6.

Wash and scrub the potatoes very thoroughly and dry completely. Toss with 3 tablespoons olive oil to coat.

Distribute the bay leaves evenly over the bottom of a heavy shallow casserole with a cover. Sprinkle with 1 tablespoon coarse salt. Place the potatoes on top and sprinkle them with 1 tablespoon coarse salt. Cover tightly, sealing with foil if necessary.

Bake for 1 hour. Remove from the oven. With a large spoon, transfer the potatoes and bay leaves to a platter. Cut the potatoes in half. Drizzle with remaining olive oil. Add additional coarse salt and freshly ground black pepper to taste.

Serves 4 to 5

Broccoli di Rape I-II-III

This leafy green vegetable with a slightly bitter taste is a favourite in our house. We look forward to its arrival and cook it in fanciful ways. Also known as broccolirab *in parts of southern Italy, it actually is the green leaves and stems of a large round turnip, correctly called* cime di rape.

I.

500 g/1 lb broccoli di rape

375 ml/12 fl oz chicken broth

60 g/2 oz sultanas

II.

500 g/1 lb broccoli di rape

60 ml/2 fl oz extra-virgin olive oil

4 small cloves garlic, sliced

III.

500 g/1 lb broccoli di rape

Half of a 60-g/2-oz tin anchovy fillets in oil

2 tablespoons pine nuts, lightly toasted

(see Note)

I. Trim the bottoms of the broccoli di rape. Wash well and pat dry with kitchen paper. Put in a heavy enamel pan with the broth and the sultanas and cook over medium heat until tender, about 15 minutes. Remove broccoli di rape with tongs. Reduce broth, add salt and pepper to taste and pour over top.

II. Trim the bottoms of the broccoli di rape. Wash well and pat dry with kitchen paper. Put olive oil and garlic in a large heavy frying pan and cook until garlic just begins to brown. Add broccoli di rape and a few tablespoons of water and cook until tender. Season with salt and pepper.

III. Trim the bottoms of the broccoli di rape. Wash well and pat dry with kitchen paper. Chop the anchovies coarsely. Put the anchovies and all their oil in the bottom of a large nonstick frying pan. Add the broccoli di rape and a few tablespoons of water. Cook over medium heat until tender. Season with pepper. Remove broccoli di rape and pan juices to platter. Top with toasted pine nuts.

I, II, III: Serves 4

Note: To toast pine nuts, put them in a small nonstick frying pan and cook 30 seconds until they turn golden. Shake pan so pine nuts do not stick or get scorched.

Chardonnay Cabbage

ADD-ONS

Garnish with a chiffonade of fresh basil leaves, or for a different taste, 2 teaspoons caraway seeds.

Slow braising in a budget-priced chardonnay gives this particularly friendless vegetable a fighting chance. Wine is a great coverup for cabbage's dreaded bouquet and mellows it into a side dish of softness and charm.

1.5 kg/3 lb green cabbage

750 ml/24 fl oz chardonnay

90 g/3 oz unsalted butter, melted

Cut the cabbage into 2-cm/¾-inch-thick slices. Soak in cold water mixed with 1 tablespoon coarse salt for 1 hour. Drain the cabbage and put it in a large, heavy saucepan. Barely cover with the wine. Cover the pan and simmer over low heat for 1½ hours.

With a slotted spoon, remove the cabbage to a large bowl. Mix with melted butter. Quickly reduce the cooking liquid until syrupy and lightly browned. Pour over the cabbage. Add salt and freshly ground pepper.

Serves 8 to 10

Two-Way Grits

Grits, made from coarsely ground hominy (dried sweetcorn kernels), are America's answer to polenta. Stone-ground grits give the best results.

I. Cheddar-Pepper
125 g/4 oz quick-cooking grits

90 g/3 oz grated mature Cheddar cheese

30 g/1 oz unsalted butter

II. Garlic
2 cloves garlic

125 g/4 oz quick-cooking grits

60 ml/2 fl oz extra-virgin olive oil

I Bring 1 litre/32 fl oz water plus 1 teaspoon salt to a boil. Slowly add grits and stir well. Lower heat, cover and cook 5 to 6 minutes, stirring twice. Remove cover and add cheese, butter and lots of freshly ground black pepper. Stir until smooth.

If desired, pour grits into shallow casserole to 2.5-cm/1-inch thickness and top with more grated cheddar. Bake at 350°C/350°F/gas 4 for 10 minutes.

II Bring 1 litre/32 fl oz water, 1 teaspoon salt, and garlic cloves, pushed through garlic press, to a boil. Slowly add grits and stir well. Lower heat, cover, and cook 5 to 6 minutes, stirring twice. Remove cover and cook 1 to 2 minutes, until thick. Stir in the olive oil. Season to taste with salt and freshly ground white pepper.

I: Unbaked—makes 1 litre/32 fl oz, serving 6 to 8
   Baked—serves 6 to 8
II: Makes 875 ml/28 fl oz, serving 6 to 8

Yucca "Hash Browns"
with Red Pepper

ADD-ONS

Serve with hot sauce
and a squeeze of lime.

If you've never been south of Florida in America, quite probably you pass by yucca in markets without ever making its acquaintance. Let me introduce you: It is one of those brown, tuberous things that you don't know what to do with but is wildly popular in Latin America and the Caribbean. This dish is so filling that you may as well forget a main course.

625 g/1¼ lb yucca

60 ml/2 fl oz vegetable oil

1 large red pepper, seeded and finely chopped

Peel the yucca with a small, sharp knife and cut it into large chunks. Remove any woody parts. Place in a medium-size pan with salted water to cover. Bring to a boil, lower heat, cover and cook for 20 to 30 minutes until soft. Drain.

Heat 3 tablespoons oil in a 25-cm/10-inch nonstick frying pan. Add yucca and chopped pepper and sauté 3 minutes. Mash with a wooden fork and cook over medium heat until golden. Turn over with a metal spatula. Add 1 tablespoon oil. With spatula, break up the pancake into pieces to look like coarse hash brown potatoes. Continue to cook until crisp all over. Season with salt and freshly ground pepper to taste. Serve hot, cut into wedges.

Serves 4 to 6

Creamed Potatoes, Swedish-Style

I love the idea of pairing hot creamed potatoes with cold smoked salmon, which they regularly do in Sweden. They drink schnapps, a shot of ice-cold aquavit or vodka.

750 g/1½ lb medium-size potatoes

30 g/1 oz unsalted butter

375 ml/12 fl oz single cream

Peel the potatoes and dice into small cubes. Melt the butter in a large nonstick frying pan and sauté potatoes for 2 minutes, being careful not to let them brown.

Pour the cream over the potatoes and add 1½ teaspoons salt. Cover and cook 20 minutes, or until the potatoes are soft.

Serves 4 to 5 as a side dish, 8 as an accompaniment to smoked salmon or gravlax

Sprinkle potatoes with finely chopped dill. You can also add 60 g/ 2 oz chopped yellow onion when potatoes are sautéed, as is the custom in southern Sweden.

Wilted Cucumbers, Dill Butter

Most people don't think about cooking cucumbers. In fact, the pale-green flesh becomes unrecognizably tender, delicate and as translucent as jade. This is a splendid use for a vegetable that otherwise has been relegated to the salad bowl.

4 large cucumbers

45 g/1½ oz unsalted butter

6 tablespoons freshly chopped dill

Peel cucumbers, cut in half lengthwise and scoop out seeds. Cut the pieces in thirds, then lengthwise into 6-mm/¼-inch-wide julienne.

Parboil in salted water for 5 minutes and drain. Keep warm in small pan, tightly covered.

Melt the butter in a frying pan. Add the cucumbers and sauté 3 minutes. Toss with the dill and add salt and pepper to taste.

Serves 6 to 8

Wild Rice and Bulgur Toss

Elegant, earthy, and sweetly divine: A grass, a grain and a grape. Serve with your Christmas turkey, roast duck or rump steak. Or use as a nutritious base for a tasty grain salad. If you have any vegans coming to dinner, serve this with grilled field mushrooms for a classy repast.

> **90 g/3 oz wild rice, uncooked**
>
> **200 g/6½ oz coarse bulgur wheat**
>
> **75 g/2½ oz currants**

Wash the rice and put it in a saucepan with 500 ml/16 fl oz water and ½ teaspoon salt. Bring to a boil. Cover the pan, lower the heat, and simmer 45 to 55 minutes, until kernels are opened and tender but not mushy. Drain excess liquid.

Meanwhile, add bulgur to a pan with 500 ml/ 16 fl oz water. Bring to a boil, cover pan, lower heat and simmer 5 minutes. Turn off heat, add currants, cover and let bulgur steam 10 minutes.

When rice is done, drain well in colander. Put in large bowl and mix gently with cooked bulgur. Add salt and freshly ground black pepper to taste. Toss with a fork to keep fluffy.

Serves 4 to 6

ADD-ONS

Drizzle with walnut oil and finely chopped spring onions.

Braised Celery Batons,
Fried Celery Leaves

"Celery raw, develops the jaw.
But celery stewed, is more quietly chewed."

I've always loved this little ditty and invented this dish to honour Ogden Nash (although I refuse to eat my peas with honey).

1 bunch celery

2 medium cloves garlic

60 ml/2 fl oz olive oil

Remove the outer stalks from the celery, leaving the tender ones inside. Reserve the leaves. Save the outer stalks for another use.

Cut the inside stalks into 5-cm/2-inch pieces and then into 6-mm/¼-inch-thick julienne. You should have about 500 g/1 lb of celery batons.

Bring a large pan of salted water to a boil. Add the celery and boil 8 minutes. Drain in a colander under cold running water.

Cut the garlic into small pieces. Heat the oil in a medium-size pan and sauté the garlic until golden, about 2 minutes. Add celery and cook 10 minutes, or until tender. Remove from the pan with a slotted spoon. Add the celery leaves and fry 1 minute (adding a little more oil, if necessary). Serve immediately.

Serves 6

Baked Sweet Fennel, Parmesan Crust

Slow baking of these pale-green bulbs—sometimes called Florence fennel or sweet fennel—brings out their natural sugars, forming a sheen of caramel. Their anise-like flavour marries well with the sweet nutty taste of real Parmigiano-Reggiano.

3 medium-size fennel bulbs

3 tablespoons fruity olive oil

6 tablespoons grated Parmigiano-Reggiano

Preheat the oven to 200°C/400°F/gas 6.

Trim the fronds and stalks off the fennel bulbs and reserve for another use. Remove any dark spots from the fennel and trim the outside layer. Cut the fennel in half lengthwise through the root.

Place the bulbs cut side up in a shallow baking dish. Sprinkle with salt and freshly ground black pepper. Drizzle each piece with 1 teaspoon olive oil.

Bake 25 minutes. Turn the bulbs over, adding a little more oil if necessary. Lower the heat to 180°C/350°F/gas 4 and bake 20 minutes longer.

Turn the fennel over so the cut side is up. Sprinkle each fennel half with 1 tablespoon grated Parmesan cheese and bake 5 minutes longer.

Serves 6

ADD-ONS

Sprinkle also with balsamic vinegar. For a trattoria-style main course, add sweet Italian sausage that has been crumbled and cooked.

Pan-Grilled Radicchio, Fried Rosemary

This pretty Italian white-veined magenta lettuce, related to chicory and endive, is at once bitter, peppery and slightly acidic. Generally used in salads, it is excellent cooked, especially pan-grilled, when it gets a nice smoky overtone.

My garnish of edible fried rosemary was unexpectedly felicitous— even to me.

2 medium-large radicchio

60 ml/2 fl oz extra-virgin olive oil

8 sprigs of fresh rosemary, each about 5 cm/
    2 inches long

Wash radicchio and remove any brown outer leaves. Cut radicchio in half lengthwise through the root end.

Heat a large nonstick frying pan. Add the radicchio cut side down and press down with a metal spatula. The radicchio will blacken and get smoky. Turn over and repeat.

Turn again so that radicchio is cut side down. Add the oil, let it get hot, and immediately add the rosemary, which will get brown and crisp.

Remove the radicchio and rosemary to a platter and pour the oil over top. Sprinkle with coarse salt and serve hot.

Serves 4

French Potato Cake

Somewhere between a Jewish latke and Swiss rösti, these potatoes are first boiled, then grated and sautéed. The result is a thick and golden potato cake—crisp on the outside, creamy on the inside.

These potatoes "take the cake" when topped with Red Wine Apple Sauce (page 287) and soured cream, or crème fraîche and smoked fish. For a distinguished hors d'oeuvre, make them into small bite-size cakes and crown them with caviar.

> **500 g/1 lb potatoes**
>
> **1 small onion**
>
> **3 tablespoons peanut oil**

Wash the potatoes and put them in a pan with water to cover. Bring to a boil, lower the heat, and cook 15 to 20 minutes, until potatoes are just turning tender. Rinse under cold water. Peel and let cool completely.

Grate the potatoes on the large holes of a hand grater. Put in a bowl. Peel the onion and grate on the large holes of the grater. You will have 1½ to 2 tablespoons onion "purée." Add the onions to the potatoes, with ½ teaspoon salt and freshly ground black pepper.

In a 20-cm/8-inch nonstick frying pan, heat 1½ tablespoons of the oil. Pack in the potato mixture and cook over medium heat for 10 minutes, or until bottom is crisp. Slide the potato cake from the pan onto a plate. Place the pan upside down over the potato cake, then turn the plate and pan over so that the cake is now cooked side up. Add remaining oil and cook 10 minutes longer, or until both sides are browned and crisp.

Serves 4

Giant Glazed Onions, Balsamic Vinegar

Since 1978 I have been guest chef at the annual grape harvest of Clinton Vineyards in New York's beautiful Hudson Valley. These glorious onions were always part of the dinner buffet of local ingredients, where the Feders' award-winning sevyal blanc was featured.

3 very large mild onions

4 tablespoons extra-virgin olive oil

3 tablespoons balsamic vinegar

Preheat the oven to 200°C/400°F/gas 6.

Peel the onions and cut them in half horizontally. Put cut side down in heavy shallow casserole. Pour 2 tablespoons of the oil over the onions. Add a sprinkling of coarse salt and freshly ground black pepper.

Bake 20 minutes. The cut side of the onions will be black. Turn them over and flatten with a metal spatula. Bake another 15 minutes. Turn again, flatten with a spatula, and bake another 20 minutes.

Remove the onions from the casserole. They should be soft and caramelized. Add the remaining 2 tablespoons oil and the vinegar to the pan. Pour the juices over the onions. Serve warm or at room temperature.

Serves 6

Crisp Aubergine Tassels

Also known as quaglie, *or quails, in Italian, small aubergines are cut so that they fan out like the bird's tail feathers. Certainly more romantic than "tassels," but then again they also look like "mops." No matter what you call them, they are lovely as a vegetable.*

4 baby Italian aubergines

Vegetable oil for frying

**Balsamic vinegar or Herbes de Provence
Vinegar (page 69)**

Wash the aubergines. Make a series of parallel cuts, about 8 mm/ ⅓ inch apart, starting 2.5 cm/1 inch from the stem to the bottom of the aubergine, slicing completely through the aubergine. Be careful to begin 2.5 cm/1 inch from the stem end so that aubergine remains intact. Roll the aubergines 90 degrees and cut again from stem to bottom.

Each aubergine will look like a tassel or mop.

Put the aubergines in salted water with a weight to keep them submerged. Soak for several hours. When ready to fry, remove from water and pat dry with kitchen paper.

Heat the oil in a large frying pan. The oil should be 2.5 to 4 cm/ 1 to 1½ inches deep. Fry the aubergines on both sides until crisp and golden brown. Do not let them get too dark. Remove them from the oil with a slotted spoon and assemble them on a platter. Sprinkle with vinegar and dust lightly with salt.

Serves 4

Oven-Roasted Asparagus, Fried Capers

In less than ten minutes you can have the most addictive asparagus you've ever encountered. An intense dose of heat keeps these spears green and snappy. Deep-fried capers add a startling accent. A wonderful Mediterranean-inspired first course or side dish.

1 kg/2 lb medium-size asparagus

4 tablespoons olive oil

45 g/1½ oz large capers, drained

Preheat the oven to 260°C/500°F/gas 9.

Trim the stems of the asparagus, cutting off the ends. Drizzle 2 tablespoons of the olive oil on a baking tray or Swiss roll tin. Place the asparagus on the tin and coat with oil. Sprinkle lightly with salt. Roast for 8 minutes and transfer to warm platter.

Meanwhile, in a small frying pan, heat the remaining 2 tablespoons oil. Fry the capers for 1 minute. Pour over the asparagus. Pass the pepper mill.

Serves 6

Saffron Orzo

Made in the style of its Northern Italian cousin, risotto alla Milanese, my orzo "giallo" also gets its luminescence from golden-orange saffron— a precious spice known for its singular flavour and exorbitant price. A little goes a very long way, and it will last a long time in your cupboard.

½ teaspoon chopped saffron threads

45 g/1½ oz unsalted butter

250 g/8 oz orzo

Bring 680 ml/22 fl oz water to a boil, let cool 5 minutes, and add saffron. Let sit 15 minutes.

In a medium-size heavy pan, melt the butter and stir in the orzo. Sauté a few minutes over medium heat, until orzo becomes golden.

Slowly add the saffron water and stir well with a wooden spoon. Add ½ teaspoon salt and freshly ground black pepper. Cover the pan and simmer for 10 minutes.

Uncover, increase the heat, and stir continuously for 5 minutes, or until all liquid is evaporated, resulting in a creamy-textured orzo.

Cover until ready to eat, then warm gently.

Serves 4 to 6

ADD-ONS

Add 30 g/1 oz grated Parmesan cheese to orzo while hot. Stir well.

Cumin-Scented Couscous

ADD-ONS

Add 60 g/2 oz finely diced courgettes and a squeeze of fresh lemon to the chicken broth. Also nice with a pinch of cinnamon.

Couscous, the pasta of North Africa and the Middle East, is processed semolina wheat formed into little seed-size "grains." Cumin seeds, when toasted, impart a musky flavour. Try the larger pearls of Israeli couscous for variety: both have great "mouth feel."

1¼ teaspoons cumin seeds

375 ml/12 fl oz homemade chicken broth
(page 96) or canned

185 g/6 oz couscous

Toast the cumin seeds lightly in a nonstick frying pan. Reserve.

In a medium saucepan, bring the chicken broth and cumin seeds to a boil. Lower the heat, add the couscous, and stir 2 or 3 minutes, until most of liquid is absorbed. Add salt and pepper. Cover. Keep warm until ready to serve.

Serves 6 to 8

Aromatic Ginger Rice

Any long-grain rice will do for this elegant sidekick, but basmati is best. Originally from India but now grown elsewhere as well, basmati rice has a lovely fragrance of its own. You'll want to keep some in your pantry.

7.5-cm/3-inch piece fresh ginger root

250 g/8 oz uncooked rice, long-grain white or basmati

30 g/1 oz unsalted butter

Peel the ginger root and mince half of it into very tiny cubes; you should have 1 tablespoon. Grate the remaining ginger on the large holes of a hand grater. Place in a piece of kitchen paper and squeeze into a small dish until you have 1 teaspoon ginger juice.

Bring 500 ml/16 fl oz of water and 1 teaspoon coarse salt to a boil. Add the rice and the 1 tablespoon minced ginger. Cover, lower heat, and simmer 20 minutes, or until water is evaporated.

Melt the butter in a small pan and add the ginger juice. Drain the rice well. Add the melted ginger-butter and freshly ground white pepper.

Serves 6

ADD-ONS

Garnish rice with 30 g/1 oz toasted pine nuts (see note on page 197).

Egg Noodles with Butter and Rosemary

ADD-ONS

I like to add 1½ table-spoons of white wine when tossing the noodles with the butter.

Use broad noodles, or pappardelle, for making this noteworthy accompaniment to simple roasts. Or collect, as I do, bits of leftover dried pasta in a large jar—a pasta potpourri—for an added dimension.

500 g/1 lb broad egg noodles

90 g/3 oz unsalted butter

1½ tablespoons fresh rosemary leaves

Bring salted water to a boil. Cook the egg noodles as directed on the package, being careful not to overcook.

Meanwhile, cut the butter into small pieces and reserve.

Snip the rosemary leaves so you have small irregular pieces, or mince with a very sharp knife.

When the noodles are cooked, drain well but do not rinse. Put in a warm bowl and toss with butter and rosemary, stirring carefully with a wooden spoon. Add salt and freshly ground black pepper to taste.

Serves 6

Orange and Gold Potato Purée, Sweet Potato Crisps

Buttermilk adds old-fashioned richness to a dish that is simplicity itself and especially grand with its garnish of crunchy sweet potato crisps. You can also bake the sweet potatoes and fill the scooped-out shells with this autumnal purée.

1 kg/2 lb large sweet potatoes

750 g/1½ lb potatoes

160 ml/5 fl oz buttermilk, at room temperature

Preheat the oven to 105°C/225°F/gas ¼.

To make the sweet potato crisps: Use 250 g/8 oz of the sweet potatoes (or half of a large sweet potato). Peel the sweet potato and slice into paper-thin rounds. Place the rounds on a large baking tray. Bake 50 minutes, turning twice. They should become crisp and take on a bit of colour. Do not let them brown. Sprinkle with salt and reserve.

To make the purée: Peel the remaining sweet potatoes and the potatoes. Cut them into large chunks and put them in a large pan with cold salted water to cover. Bring to a boil, lower heat, and cook 30 minutes, or until potatoes are very soft. Drain the water.

Mash the potatoes with a potato masher or put them through a ricer. Mix well, adding buttermilk until potatoes are creamy and smooth. Add salt and pepper to taste. Reheat gently before serving, adding 1 or 2 tablespoons buttermilk if needed. Stick sweet potato crisps into purée.

Serves 6 to 8

Husk-Roasted Sweetcorn, Chilli Butter

This unique method for cooking sweetcorn is especially good for a crowd. Blackening the husk imparts campfire flavour, while chilli powder adds a smoky aroma. These look especially grand on a platter with the papery husks peeled back, giving you something to hold on to.

I wonder why they're called ears.

60 g/2 oz unsalted butter

1 teaspoon good-quality chilli powder

6 large ears of sweetcorn, in husks

Let the butter soften slightly. Mix well with chilli powder and ¼ teaspoon salt. Roll into the shape of a small log, 2.5 cm/1 inch in diameter (or put into a small ramekin). Refrigerate until firm.

Preheat the grill. Sprinkle husks with water and place the sweetcorn on a baking tray. Grill on all sides until husks turn black.

Heat the oven to 260°C/500°F/gas 9 and roast for 5 minutes. Peel back the husks with a clean tea towel, keeping the husk attached to the sweetcorn cob. Serve with thin slices of the chilli butter.

Serves 6

Perfect Mashed Potatoes

Three ingredients never tasted so luxurious. These potatoes are so sinful, they're almost a sauce. Spending a few extra minutes pushing the potatoes through a sieve gives them ultra-smooth finesse. Fabulous topped with freshly steamed spinach kissed with lemon.

1 kg/2 lb potatoes

155 g/5 oz unsalted butter, cold

180 ml/6 fl oz single cream

Scrub the potatoes but do not peel them. Place in a pan with salted water to cover by 2.5 cm/1 inch. Bring to a boil, lower heat, and simmer 30 minutes, or until tender. Drain immediately. Peel the potatoes when they are cool enough to handle.

Using a food mill or a potato masher, mash the potatoes well. Incorporate the butter bit by bit, stirring with a wooden spoon.

Heat the cream and slowly add it to potatoes. Season to taste with sea salt and freshly ground white pepper.

Pass the mixture through a large, fine sieve, using a large spoon, into a medium-size saucepan. Loosen with a few tablespoons cold water if necessary. Heat gently.

Serves 6 or more

ADD-ONS

Also delicious drizzled with vibrant Parsley Juice (page 218).

Parsley Juice

1 large bunch Italian parsley
2 tablespoons extra-virgin olive oil

Remove the leaves from the parsley. Blanch in boiling water for 1 minute. Plunge in cold water and drain. Purée in blender with 60 ml/2 fl oz cold water and oil. Process until smooth. Season to taste and strain through sieve.

Makes about 375 ml/12 fl oz

Tender White Beans with Tarragon

White beans are a wonderful foil for the singular taste of fresh tarragon. In a gossamer dressing of fragrant, green oil and a little cooking liquid, this salad/side dish satisfies—hot or cold.

500 g/1 lb white cannellini beans

4½ tablespoons extra-virgin olive oil

2 tablespoons coarsely chopped fresh
  tarragon leaves

Soak the beans in cold water for a minimum of 12 hours. Make sure beans are covered by 5 cm/2 inches of water.

Drain the beans, rinse them well, and put in large heavy pan with water to cover. Add ½ teaspoon whole black peppercorns. Bring to a boil and let boil rapidly for 2 minutes, skimming any white foam from the top.

Lower the heat and simmer gently, uncovered, for 1¾ to 2 hours, until beans are tender but not mushy and falling apart. Add more water during cooking to keep the beans covered.

Drain the beans in a colander, saving 60 ml/2 fl oz of cooking liquid. Put the beans in a large bowl. Add olive oil and reserved cooking liquid.

Add coarse salt to taste, about 1½ teaspoons, and a pinch of white pepper. Add the tarragon and mix well. Serve hot or at room temperature, adding more olive oil, if desired.

Serves 8 to 10

Ultra Tomatoes

Here are two methods for maximizing the flavour of tomatoes. The slow evaporation of moisture gives even pallid fruit a sweet, meaty taste. Slow-roasted tomatoes are not quite as dried as sun-dried—they have a distinctive texture and intensity of their own. This bright addition to salads and pastas makes monochromatic main courses come alive.

ADD-ONS

Toss a handful of fresh thyme or rosemary over the tomatoes before baking.

I. Slow-Roasted Plum Tomatoes

12 plum tomatoes, halved lengthwise

3 tablespoons extra-virgin olive oil

3 cloves garlic, finely chopped

Preheat oven to 120°C/250°F/gas ½.

Place the tomatoes cut side up in a single layer on a baking tray (you can line the tray with greaseproof paper).

Heat the oil in a small frying pan. Add the chopped garlic and sauté 1 minute. Drizzle the oil and garlic over the tomatoes and sprinkle lightly with coarse salt.

Place the tomatoes in the oven and bake for 2½ to 3 hours. The tomatoes should retain their shape. Let cool.

II. Melted Tomatoes

12 large ripe red tomatoes

3 tablespoons olive oil

6 large cloves garlic

Preheat the oven to 120°C/250°F/gas ½.

Bring a pan of water to a boil and boil the tomatoes for 1 minute. Drain and peel. Cut in half and seed. Put them on a foil-lined baking tray, cut side down. Drizzle with oil. Sprinkle lightly with sea salt. Sprinkle a few cloves of crushed garlic over. Bake for 4 hours.

I, II: Makes 24 pieces

Chapter 11

Desserts and Other Sweet Things

Desserts are designed to tease. They are the ultimate temptation when one's appetite has largely been satisfied.

I'm not one who craves a sweet every day, but I simply swoon when the words "bonbon," "confection" or "confiture" come to mind.

Words like "candied" and "nectarous," "sugar-coated" and "honeyed," make me weak.

Images from long ago, like the brick of melting ice cream in Candy Land, transform me. Simple ideas like chocolate-covered cherries make me delirious.

Desserts are for when we go over the top.

Vanilla Sugar

1 kg/2 lb granulated sugar
2 vanilla pods

Put the sugar in a large bowl. Split the vanilla pods in half lengthwise. With the tip of a knife, scrape out the vanilla seeds, reserving the pods, and add them to the sugar. Mix well with the fingertips, making sure the vanilla seeds are well distributed—they are moist and tend to stick together. Place the sugar in a large jar with the open vanilla pods. Cover tightly and store in a cool, dark place.

Makes 1 kg/2 lb

Cinnamon Sugar

500 g/1 lb granulated sugar
30 g/1 oz good-quality ground cinnamon

Mix the sugar and cinnamon together in a bowl until thoroughly blended. Cover tightly and store in a cool, dark place.

Makes 500 g/1 lb

Green Apple and Lychee Tart

Fragrant and haunting, green apples and lychees make a compelling team on top of crisp and buttery puff pastry pillows. The syrup from the lychees is reduced and used as a burnishing glaze. Serve with a cup of steamy green tea.

1 sheet frozen puff pastry, defrosted (about 250 g/8 oz)

1 (375-g/12-oz) can lychee nuts, in heavy syrup

2 Granny Smith apples

Preheat the oven to 190°C/375°F/gas 5.

Cut the puff pastry into 4 equal 13-cm/5-inch squares. You may need to roll out dough slightly with a rolling pin. Keep it cold while you prepare the topping.

Drain the lychees well in a sieve, saving all the juice. Put the juice in a small heavy saucepan and reserve.

Cut the lychees in half and place them evenly on the pastry squares, leaving a 12-mm/½-inch border. The lychees should completely cover the centres of the pastry squares.

Peel the apples. Core and seed them and slice them into very thin wedges. Arrange the slices in an overlapping pattern on top of the lychees. Arrange the squares on an ungreased baking tray.

Bake for 15 to 20 minutes, until edges of pastry have puffed.

Meanwhile, reduce the syrup in the saucepan until it becomes a dark brown, thick glaze.

Glaze the tarts lightly with the reduced syrup, using a pastry brush, and bake 10 minutes longer. The pastry will be golden brown.

Remove the tarts from the oven. Brush with any remaining glaze.

Serve warm or at room temperature within 3 hours of baking.

Sprinkle 1 teaspoon Cinnamon Sugar (page 224) on top of each tart after initial glazing.

GRAPENOTE

Serve tart warm with a small glass of chilled Muscat de Beaumes-de-Venise or an Alsace late-harvest riesling.

Serve with ice cream or with whipped cream, if desired, especially if cutting in half to serve 8.

Makes 4 individual tarts, serving 4 or 8

Frozen Maple Soufflé

As if life weren't hectic enough, guests are coming for dinner tonight! Here's an easy but elegant dessert you can serve with confidence. Its dulcet taste is worth every ounce of the costly maple syrup.

1 scant tablespoon powdered gelatine

500 ml/16 fl oz maple syrup

500 ml/16 fl oz double cream, whipped

Dissolve the gelatine in 125 ml/4 fl oz cold water. Bring the maple syrup to a boil. Lower the heat and add the gelatine. Cook 2 minutes while stirring. Let stand until mixture begins to thicken. Slowly fold syrup into whipped cream, folding in well after each addition. Pour into parfait glasses and freeze.

Or you can put the mixture in a prepared 1-litre/32-fl oz soufflé dish fitted with a foil collar, or in a nonstick 20-cm/8-inch loaf tin, and freeze.

Serves 6

ADD-ONS

Garnish with crushed Almond Brittle from Sicily (page 269) or sprinkle with miniature plain chocolate drops. If serving from a loaf tin, slice thick and drizzle with Chocolate Maple Syrup (page 228).

Chocolate Maple Syrup

125 ml/4 fl oz pure maple syrup
2 tablespoons cocoa powder
30 g/1 oz unsalted butter

In a small saucepan, heat the syrup until hot. Remove the pan from the heat. Whisk in cocoa and butter until the mixture is smooth.

Makes 150 ml/5 fl oz

Dark Chocolate Mousse

Mild obsession with a particular style of chocolate mousse is probably normal—and as personal and profound as the way one drinks coffee. I like my coffee black, my chocolate mousse intense.

4 extra-large eggs, separated

220 g/7 oz excellent-quality dark chocolate

80 ml/3 fl oz hot, strong coffee

Separate the eggs. Chop the chocolate into small pieces. Place the chocolate, coffee, and egg yolks in a blender and blend thoroughly.

Beat the egg whites with a pinch of salt until stiff. Fold the egg whites with the chocolate mixture. Mix gently but thoroughly.

Pour the mousse into a soufflé dish. Chill. Garnish with grated chocolate if desired.

Serves 6 to 8

ADD-ONS

Serve with rum-flavoured whipped cream.

Alice B. Toklas's Sugar Candy

ADD-ONS

Scatter the top of the "candy" with finely chopped nuts before it cools.

I first encountered this recipe in the Alice B. Toklas Cookbook, *published in 1954. Alice, of course, was lover, confidante and constant dining companion to the celebrated writer Gertrude Stein. According to Alice, "During the war there was a shortage of sugar, however this simple candy remained a staple of our household." Making this confection is like watching paint dry, but the results are well worth it.*

250 ml/8 fl oz double cream

250 g/8 oz granulated sugar

1 teaspoon brandy

Put the ingredients in an enamel saucepan over low heat and stir constantly with a wooden spoon until the mixture is the colour of coffee with cream. This will take 45 to 50 minutes.

Remove from the flame and pour onto an oiled marble slab or into a small nonstick square or rectangular tin so that the candy is 8-mm/⅓-inch thick. Cool 20 minutes and cut into small squares.

Makes 24 to 32 pieces

Lemon Buttermilk Ice Cream

How luxurious only 2 grams of fat can taste!

440 g/14 oz caster sugar

6 large lemons

1 litre/32 fl oz buttermilk

Put the sugar in a medium-size bowl. Grate the zest of 2 or 3 lemons so that you have 2 tablespoons of zest. Juice as many lemons as needed to get 125 ml/4 fl oz lemon juice. Add zest and juice to the sugar in the bowl and mix well.

Add the buttermilk and ⅛ teaspoon coarse salt and stir until sugar is dissolved. Chill 4 hours or overnight. Freeze in an ice-cream maker according to the manufacturer's instructions.

Serves 8

ADD-ONS

Serve on Strawberries in Grappa (page 232).

GRAPENOTES

Sensational with a glass of Asti Spumante.

Strawberries in Grappa

The fire of grappa is softened here by the juice of sweet berries. Crowned with Lemon Buttermilk Ice Cream and a tuft of opal basil, this becomes a "sundae" for adults.

ADD-ONS

Garnish with sprigs of opal basil, lemon balm or fresh mint. Delicious with Lemon Buttermilk Ice Cream (page 231) or a quenelle-shaped oval of mascarpone cheese.

> 750 g/1½ lb ripe fresh strawberries
>
> 1½ tablespoons sugar
>
> 60 ml/2 fl oz grappa

One hour before serving, wash the berries and remove the stems. Cut the large berries into quarters and the small berries in half. Place in a bowl. Toss with the sugar, the grappa and a grinding of black pepper. Chill 1 hour.

Serves 4

Corsetière's Despair

This peppermint-speckled frozen folly dates back to 1949—and looks it. It makes magic as it melts in your mouth and is as invigorating as a tumble in freshly fallen snow. A few drops of red food colouring slashed through the mixture with a knife produce swirls of brilliant red and soft hues of pink.

ADD-ONS
Serve with lashings of your favourite hot fudge sauce.

> 500 g/1 lb red-and-white-striped peppermint
>   sugar canes
>
> 1 litre/32 fl oz double cream
>
> 3 or 4 drops red food colouring

Coarsely chop one-third of the sugar canes and reserve. Grind the remainder in a food processor until it is a fine powder.

Whip the cream with pinch of salt in large chilled bowl until stiff. Fold all the powdered sugar canes and about half of the coarse pieces into the cream. Add the red food colouring, slashing through with knife to make red streaks.

Prepare a 2-litre/64-fl oz soufflé dish with a foil collar: Fold a 90-cm/3-foot length of foil in half lengthwise and wrap the soufflé dish with the foil; either tie the foil or hold it in place by folding its two ends together. Fill with the mixture and add remaining coarse sugar canes on top. Freeze until hard, about 3 hours. Remove foil and serve. You also can make individual-size soufflés, which will freeze faster.

Serves 8 to 10

Pastel Easter Sorbet
(Kiwi and Galia Melon)

ADD-ONS

Drizzle each serving
with 1 tablespoon
crème de cassis or
green chartreuse
liqueur. Or you can
add ½ tablespoon of
each. For kids, top
with a few colourful
jelly beans.

*Over exposed by the oddities of nouvelle cuisine, the kiwi is nonetheless
an adorable fruit with good acidity and sweetness and decorative little
seeds. Coupled with the intense perfume of a Galia melon from Israel,
or the Cavaillon from France, it makes a simple water ice sublime.
Substitute half of a ripe honeydew melon for the Galia, if you must.*

185 g/6 oz sugar

1 ripe Galia melon

3 kiwi fruit

Place water in small saucer and 60 g/2 oz of the sugar in another
small saucer. Select six large white-wine glasses and dip their rims
first in the water and then in the sugar. Repeat the process and place
the glasses in the freezer.

Peel the Galia melon and the kiwi. Remove any seeds and membranes from the melon. Cut the fruit into 2.5-cm/1-inch chunks and
add to a food processor with pinch of salt. Purée until smooth. You
should have 750 ml/24 fl oz. Reserve.

In a small saucepan, boil the remaining sugar and 125 ml/4 fl oz
water for 2 minutes. Let cool.

Mix the fruit purée and sugar syrup. Chill several hours. Put into
an ice cream maker and proceed according to the manufacturer's
instructions. Spoon into prepared wine glasses and freeze.

Serves 6

Chocolate Bread Pudding

It's rare to have leftover breakfast chocolate croissants, since they're hard to resist. But it's worth the restraint so you can make this newfangled bread pudding for lunch or dinner.

2 or 3 large day-old pain au chocolat

375 ml/12 fl oz chocolate milk

2 extra-large eggs

Preheat the oven to 180°C/350°F/gas 4.

Slice the pain au chocolat into 12-mm/½-inch slices. Let dry 30 minutes, then place in a 1-litre/32-fl oz porcelain soufflé dish. The bread should fill the dish.

In a mixer, blend the milk, the eggs and a pinch of salt until fluffy. Pour the mixture over the pain au chocolat, pressing the bread gently so that the milk covers the top. Let sit 5 minutes.

Bake 40 to 45 minutes. The bread pudding will look like a soufflé but will deflate as it cools. Serve slightly warm, or chilled if desired.

Serves 2

ADD-ONS

Add 90 g/3 oz of chocolate drops to mixture before baking. Serve with sweetened whipped cream dusted with cocoa powder. Delicious with a scoop of Bittersweet Cocoa Sorbet (page 248).

Iced Maple Custard,
Warm Maple Syrup

This is crème caramel without the "caramel" (melted sugar) but rather with pure maple syrup acting as both a sweetener and a sauce. Its jolt of contrasts—cold, creamy custard anointed with warm, sticky sweetness—pleases the senses.

3 extra-large eggs, beaten

180 ml/6 fl oz pure maple syrup

500 ml/16 fl oz single cream

Preheat the oven to 180°C/350°F/gas 4.

Combine the beaten eggs, 125 ml/4 fl oz of the maple syrup, the cream and a pinch of salt. Pour the mixture into large glass custard cups.

Set the cups in a flat tin with sides as high as the cups and put the tin in the oven. Carefully pour very hot water to a depth of about half the cups' height. Bake 40 minutes, or until custards are just set. Let cool and refrigerate until very cold.

When ready to serve, gently warm the remaining maple syrup and serve drizzled on top. Or turn custards out of cups onto plates and drizzle syrup around the edges.

Serves 4

Black Walnut Bars

It was from my boss, the legendary New York restaurateur Joe Baum, that I learned about black walnuts. Here I combine these funky-smelling nuts in a confection something like a brownie. You will crave a glass of milk.

185 g/6 oz crushed digestive biscuits

185 g/6 oz coarsely chopped black walnuts (see Note)

1 (440-g/14-oz) can sweetened condensed milk

Preheat the oven to 180°C/350°F/gas 4.

Put the digestive crumbs and walnuts in a medium-size bowl. Slowly add the condensed milk and a pinch of salt. Mix with a wooden spoon. Mixture will be very thick and gooey.

Pack into a nonstick 20-cm/8-inch square tin, or into a 35-cm/9½-inch round removable-bottom tin lined with greaseproof paper. Wet your hands with cold water and smooth the dough on top.

Bake for 30 to 35 minutes. Let cool. Wrap the leftover cake very well in cling film or foil. Keeps for weeks.

Serves 16

ADD-ONS

Add 1 teaspoon freshly grated orange zest. Also nice with 185 g/6 oz chocolate drops or yogurt-covered raisins added to the batter.

GRAPENOTE

Have a small glass of oloroso sherry.

Note: You can substitute toasted plain walnuts for black walnuts. To toast, place on a shallow tin in a 180°C/350°F/gas 4 oven for 5 minutes.

Chocolate Banana Terrine

This four-star recipe underscores the simple and sublime philosophy of Recipes 1-2-3: easy to make, great to look at, decadent to eat.

Serve with a dollop of vanilla ice cream and toasted slivered almonds.

Nice with a glass of velvety Madeira.

> **5 small to medium ripe bananas, peeled**
>
> **250 ml/8 fl oz double cream**
>
> **500 g/1 lb excellent-quality bittersweet chocolate, chopped in small pieces**

Line a 20-by 10-cm/ 8- by 4-inch loaf tin with cling film. Place the bananas in the tin to make 2 layers. In a small saucepan, bring the cream to a boil and melt the chocolate in the cream, stirring constantly with a wooden spoon. When the chocolate is completely melted and the mixture is smooth, pour it over the bananas. Let cool, then refrigerate overnight.

Unmould, remove cling film and serve in one 12-mm/½-inch-thick slice or two thinner slices.

Optional: Purée one very ripe banana with a few tablespoons of water until very smooth. Serve alongside the terrine.

Serves 12

Prune Jelly with Prune Kernels

From the cutting-edge 20th Century Cookbook, *published in 1897 in Rochester, New York, comes this mildly sinister recipe. Once you've mastered the arcane art of separating prune kernels from their shells, it may become your "regular" dessert.*

> 500 g/1 lb prunes with stones
>
> 125 g/4 oz sugar
>
> 1 scant tablespoon powdered gelatine

Stone the prunes and reserve the stones. Put the prunes, the sugar and water to cover in a saucepan and cook over low heat for 2 hours. (Original recipe: While prunes are cooking, soak prune stones in boiling water for 30 minutes. Drain and reserve.)

Pass the prunes through a mesh sieve or a food mill, or purée until smooth in a food processor.

Soak the gelatine in 2 tablespoons cold water and add to prunes. (Original recipe: With the side of a big knife, break open the prune stones, remove the kernels, and add them to the prune jelly.)

Boil together for 2 minutes and pour into a 1-litre/32-fl oz mould. Chill 2 hours, unmould and serve.

Serves 6 to 8

ADD-ONS

You can substitute red wine for water when simmering the prunes. Serve with freshly whipped cream sweetened with icing sugar and $1/4$ teaspoon almond essence.

GRAPENOTE

A small snifter of Armagnac gives this dessert a lot of class.

Fresh Blueberries,
Lemon Curd Cream

ADD-ONS

Serve with Twice-
Baked Oatcakes (page
32) for an amazing
dessert combo.

The great food philosopher Curnonsky said, "Cuisine is when things taste like themselves." In season, then, this surely must be it!

250 ml/8 fl oz double cream

125 ml/4 fl oz lemon curd

1kg/2 lb blueberries, picked over and washed

In a large chilled bowl, whip the cream by hand using a wire whisk. Whip until thick but still flowing (be careful not to overbeat). Fold in the lemon curd with a rubber spatula. Chill.

Serve over blueberries, saving some berries for a garnish.

Serves 6

Chocolate Milk Pudding

Make this in the evening and eat it warm out of the pan. Save one portion for breakfast the next day.

45 g/1½ oz cornflour

Scant 20 g/¾ oz cocoa powder

600 ml/1 pint chocolate milk

In a heavy small-size saucepan, stir together the cornflour and the cocoa powder. Slowly add the milk and stir in a pinch of salt. With a wooden spoon, stir slowly over medium heat, continually scraping the sides and bottom of the saucepan and breaking up lumps.

When mixture is smooth and beginning to thicken, stir more vigorously (you may decide to use a wire whisk at this point), lowering heat if necessary, and beat until very smooth and thick. Remove from heat and continue to stir 30 seconds. Pour into wine glasses or coffee cups.

Makes 600 ml/1 pint, serving 5

ADD-ONS

Serve with sweetened whipped cream sprinkled with cocoa powder.

Chianti Granita

A granita is a coarse-textured sorbet, reminiscent of what are sometimes called "Italian ices." Traditionally made with coffee or fresh lemon juice, this version made with Chianti (or any other full-bodied Italian wine) is my gift to chefs everywhere. It is also a great way to use leftover wine!

500 ml/16 fl oz Chianti

6 tablespoons fresh orange juice

220 g/7 oz sugar

Put the Chianti, orange juice and sugar and 600 ml/1 pint water in a heavy, nonreactive saucepan and simmer 2 to 3 minutes, until sugar is dissolved. Let cool.

Divide the mixture into two flan tins. Put in freezer. After 20 minutes, stir with a spoon, starting around the edges (this is where it freezes first). Repeat this process every 15 to 20 minutes (about 6 times) until mixture is frozen.

Scrape the surface of the frozen liquid with a spoon and put into chilled wine glasses.

Serves 6

Raspberry Cloud Soufflé

Soufflés scream "special occasion" to me, but this deceptively simple preparation is practical for everyday eating because it is remarkably low in fat! On fancy restaurant menus, soufflés are often expensive. This pink, sweet cloud is also cheap to make.

> 6 extra-large eggs
>
> 250 g/4 oz sugar
>
> 375 g/12 oz good-quality raspberry jam, with seeds

Preheat the oven to 200°C/400°F/gas 6.

Separate the eggs, reserving 1 egg yolk and the 6 egg whites (save the remaining yolks for another use). Mix the egg yolk with 2 tablespoons of the sugar and brush the inside of a 1.5-litre/2½-pint soufflé dish with the egg yolk mixture. Set aside.

Melt the jam with 2 tablespoons water. Heat gently and keep warm.

Stiffly beat the egg whites with the remaining sugar until glossy. Using a rubber spatula, fold a quarter of whites into the warm jam. Then add this mixture to the remaining whites, folding gently.

Prepare the soufflé dish with a 7.5-cm/3-inch foil collar: Fold a 60-cm/2-foot length of foil in half lengthwise; wrap the soufflé dish with the foil; either tie the foil or hold it in place by folding its two ends together. Spoon in the mixture and bake 15 to 18 minutes. Remove collar and serve immediately.

Serves 6

Add-Ons

Add 1 to 2 tablespoons kirsch or crème de cassis to jam while warming.

Grapenote

Serve with a kir royale (champagne and crème de cassis) or sweet Vouvray.

Green Melon Zabaglione

Andrew Wilkinson, once chef at the Rainbow Room in New York, developed this twist on the traditional Italian version made with marsala. It has a pleasing chartreuse colour, and its taste mystifies.

6 extra-large egg yolks

6 tablespoons sugar

6 tablespoons melon liqueur

In a double boiler, or in a bowl set over simmering water, beat the egg yolks and sugar with a wire whisk until they are light, fluffy and lemon-coloured. Continue to beat, slowly adding liqueur. Cook until thickened. The consistency should be like whipped cream.

Let custard cool a few minutes, whisk again, and pour into small wine glasses. Serve warm or chilled.

Serves 6

THE FOLLOWING PHOTOS DEPICT:

Desserts and Other Sweet Things

1. Yogurt "Coeur à la Crème," Apricot Compote
2. Corsetière's Despair
3. Strawberry Summer Pudding
4. Eggnog and Panettone Bread Pudding
5. Little Lemons Filled with Lemon Yogurt "Gelato";
   Pepper Lime Ice Cream; Amaretto "Creamsicle" in Frozen Oranges
6. Green Apple and Lychee Tart
7. Chocolate Banana Terrine
8. Turkish Cherry Bread

ADD-ONS

This custard is delicious served over a salad of chilled melon balls (honeydew, cantaloupe, Crenshaw) sprinkled with lime juice.

Maple Mousse Parfait

According to legend, American Smith College girls in the early 1900s were fond of this. But it's a comforting dessert any generation will enjoy.

3 extra-large eggs, separated

125 ml/4 fl oz pure maple syrup

250 ml/8 fl oz double cream, whipped and chilled

Beat the yolks with an electric mixer until fluffy and lemon-coloured, about 5 minutes. Add the maple syrup and cook in the top of a double boiler until the mixture becomes very thick, stirring often. Let cool completely.

Beat the egg whites with ⅛ teaspoon salt until quite stiff. Gently combine the cooled syrup mixture, egg whites and whipped double cream until thoroughly incorporated.

Spoon into beautiful parfait or martini glasses. Chill.

Serves 6

ADD-ONS

Garnish with bitter-sweet chocolate shavings or candied violets.

Syrian Shortbread

Known as grabie *in its native Syria, this shortbread belongs in biscuit jars everywhere. It is easier than traditional shortbread, just as buttery and more tender.*

ADD-ONS

Delicious with a tall glass of Iced Bedouin Coffee (opposite).

250 g/8 oz unsalted butter, at room temperature

155 g/5 oz icing sugar

315 g/10 oz plain flour

Preheat the oven to 150°C/300°F/gas 2.

In the bowl of an electric mixer, cream the butter until light and fluffy. Add the sugar gradually, and cream thoroughly. Stir in the flour and add a pinch of salt. Continue to mix until a smooth ball of dough is formed.

Roll out the dough about 6-mm/¼-inch thick on a board lightly coated with flour. Cut with a "doughnut-shaped" cutter 6 cm/ 2½ inches in diameter, or use any decorative biscuit cutter you desire. Bake on an ungreased baking tray for about 25 minutes, or until the biscuits are dry but pale in colour. Remove from the baking tray only when the biscuits have cooled.

Makes 3 dozen

Iced Bedouin Coffee

Traditional Arabic coffee is served hot, black and sweet. Usually prepared over an open fire in a special pot called a finjan, *it can also be made in large quantities in a medium-size saucepan, preferably one with a pouring spout. For hot summer days, I love this intensely flavoured coffee served chilled over ice.*

125 g/4 oz French roast coffee beans
½ tablespoon green cardamom pods
Sugar to taste (optional)

Grind the coffee beans and cardamom together until very finely ground, almost powdery. Or buy Turkish coffee at a speciality coffee shop or Middle Eastern food shop. Bring 1 litre/32 fl oz water to a boil. Add 8 tablespoons ground coffee and stir quickly with the handle of a wooden spoon. Lower the heat and let the coffee come to a boil. As the foam starts to form and come to the top of the pot, yank the pot from the heat. Add sugar, if desired, and let cool. Strain coffee through a fine-mesh sieve and refrigerate until cold. Serve over ice.

Serves 6

Bittersweet Cocoa Sorbet

A sorbet with a winning texture and elegant flavour.

125 g/4 oz sugar (or Vanilla Sugar, see
page 224)

60 g/2 oz cocoa powder

125 g/4 oz unsweetened or bittersweet
chocolate, chopped in small pieces

In a medium-size saucepan, combine 330 ml/14 fl oz water and the sugar. Bring to a boil. Whisk in the cocoa and chocolate.

When the mixture returns to a boil, remove from the heat and strain into a bowl. Let cool. Cover and refrigerate until very cold.

Process in an ice-cream maker according to the manufacturer's instructions.

Serves 4

Grate the zest of
1 orange into the
mixture. Or add 45 g/
1½ oz dark raisins
soaked in whisky.

Eggnog and Panettone Bread Pudding

A winter wonderland kind of dessert, since eggnog usually appears in shops just in time for the first frost.

> **250 g/8 oz panettone**
>
> **500 ml/16 fl oz eggnog plus 250 ml/8 fl oz for sauce (see Note)**
>
> **2 extra-large eggs**

Preheat the oven to 180°C/350°F/gas 4.

Cut the panettone into 2-cm/¾-inch cubes. Put them on a baking tray and toast them lightly in the oven. Watch carefully. The panettone should become golden, not brown.

Beat the 500 ml/16 fl oz eggnog and the eggs together using an electric mixer. Place the toasted panettone cubes in a 20-cm/8-inch square baking dish. A glass dish is preferable. Pour the eggnog mixture over the panettone, pressing down so that the panettone is submerged. Let sit 15 minutes.

Place pan in a hot-water bath (bain-marie). Bake 40 minutes. Remove from oven and let cool. Serve at room temperature or cold.

To make the sauce: Put 250 ml/8 fl oz eggnog in a small, heavy saucepan. Bring to a boil, reduce the heat and simmer very slowly, stirring often, until the sauce is reduced to 125 ml/4 fl oz and is dark tan in colour. This will take 30 to 35 minutes. Let cool. Drizzle the pudding with sauce.

Serves 6

Note: Eggnog is a traditional American Christmas drink made from a blend of milk or cream, beaten eggs, sugar, nutmeg and usually some alcohol like rum or brandy. It is available in some large supermarkets and speciality shops at Christmas time.

Oven-Roasted Strawberries, Fresh Strawberry Sorbet

ADD-ONS

Add seeds of 1 vanilla pod on top of strawberries before roasting. Garnish with lavender or mint.

GRAPENOTE

Splash Absolut Kurant over the sorbet.

In these days of oven-roasting everything for maximum flavour, American chef Daniel Boulud has taken to putting giant berries in the oven. Great idea! He serves his with ice cream; I serve mine with sorbet. Either way, the very-berry essence of warm strawberries and icy frozen fruit provides a jovial blast.

ROASTED STRAWBERRIES
30 very large strawberries, stems removed

15 g/½ oz unsalted butter, melted

3 tablespoons sugar

STRAWBERRY SORBET
500 g/1 lb ripe strawberries

60 g/3 oz caster sugar

Juice of 1 lemon

To roast the strawberries: Preheat the oven to 200°C/400°F/gas 6. Place the strawberries, side by side, stem end down, in a baking dish. Add 1 tablespoon water to the dish. Brush the berries with the melted butter and sprinkle with sugar. Bake for 6 to 8 minutes, until the berries are soft. Serve warm with pan juices. Or serve with strawberry sorbet.

To make the sorbet: Remove the stems from the berries. Place in a food processor with 250 ml/8 fl oz water, the sugar and the lemon juice. Purée until smooth, strain and freeze in an ice-cream maker according to the manufacturer's instructions.

Serves 6

"Love of Three Oranges"

    I. Orange Ambrosia

    II. Marsala Oranges with Toasted Pine Nuts

    III. Orange, Walnut and Pomegranate Salad

Love of Three Oranges is an opera by Prokofiev and has nothing to do with fruit, but I've always loved the image. My affection for these three orange recipes, however, is all about fruit and the combining of flavours with clarity and interest.

I. Orange Ambrosia

6 navel oranges

60 ml/2 fl oz Grand Marnier

60 g/2 oz unsweetened shredded coconut

Slice the ends off the oranges. Remove all the peel with a sharp knife. Slice the peeled oranges 6 mm/¼ inch thick, remove the seeds, and arrange the orange slices on a platter. Sprinkle with Grand Marnier and chill 1 hour. Let the orange slices come to room temperature before serving. Sprinkle with the shredded coconut.

ADD-ONS

Serve with amaretti biscuits.

II. Marsala Oranges with Toasted Pine Nuts

8 large oranges or blood oranges

6 tablespoons marsala wine

30 g/1 oz pine nuts, lightly toasted

Remove the skin from the oranges with a small sharp knife, leaving no white pith. Cut the oranges into segments, removing all the inner membranes. Put in a bowl and toss with the marsala.

Arrange the segments on dessert plates and sprinkle with the toasted pine nuts.

III. Orange, Walnut and Pomegranate Salad

This orange salad, which I use as a taste bridge between savoury and sweet courses, is itself savoury and sweet, with a coating of chopped walnuts and pomegranate molasses. It is also a refreshing dessert.

8 navel oranges, chilled

125 g/4 oz walnuts, toasted lightly and coarsely chopped

2 tablespoons pomegranate molasses (see Note)

With a serrated knife, cut away the orange peels and pith, discarding them, and cut the oranges crosswise into thin slices. Arrange the orange slices decoratively on a platter, overlapping slightly. The

ADD-ONS

Mix 3 tablespoons icing sugar with 1 teaspoon ground cinnamon and sift over the walnuts. Or garnish the salad with pomegranate seeds.

oranges can be prepared up to this point 4 hours ahead and chilled, covered with cling film.

In a small bowl, stir the walnuts and pomegranate molasses together well. Cover the oranges with this mixture.

I: Serves 6
II and III: Serves 8

Note: Available at speciality-food shops.

Cold Rhubarb Soup,
Mascarpone "Quenelle"

Sometime in the 1980s, fruit soups became popular desserts in fashion-able restaurants. But they've been popular in many Eastern European countries for centuries. Refreshing, beautiful and very spring-like. They are better for you than pie.

> 875 g/1¾ lb rhubarb (about 750 g/1½ lb trimmed)
>
> 185 g/6 oz Vanilla Sugar (page 224)—or more (optional)
>
> 250 g/8 oz mascarpone

Remove all the leaves from the rhubarb. Trim the stalks, wash them and pat dry. Carefully cut the rhubarb into 6-mm/¼-inch cubes.

Bring 500 ml/16 fl oz water and the sugar to a boil. Boil 1 minute, add rhubarb and return to a boil. Lower the heat. Add a pinch of salt and a pinch of freshly ground black pepper. Simmer 10 minutes. Add 1 to 2 tablespoons additional vanilla sugar if you like it sweet. Simmer 1 minute longer. Let cool and refrigerate until very cold.

Ladle the soup into soup plates. Make quenelle shapes or egg shapes from mascarpone using 2 large tablespoons. Place one on top of each bowl of soup.

Serves 6

Vanilla Sugar "Cigars"

Since no one's smoking these days, why not serve sweet cigars that you can eat? Have fun rolling your own.

90 g/3 oz unsalted butter, melted

12 sheets filo pastry

185 g/6 oz Vanilla Sugar or Cinnamon Sugar (page 224)

Preheat the oven to 180°C/350°F/gas 4.

Brush melted butter lightly over each of 12 filo sheets. Sprinkle each sheet with 2 teaspoons of the sugar.

Roll each sheet tightly to make a "cigar" that is 28 cm/11 inches long and 12 mm/½ inch wide. Brush with additional melted butter to cover the top of each cigar. Sprinkle each evenly with 1 teaspoon sugar.

Place on an ungreased baking tray and bake 15 minutes, or until golden and crisp.

Makes 12

ADD-ONS

Add 2 tablespoons instant espresso to 185 g/6 oz Vanilla Sugar and use the mixture to make Espresso Cigars. To 185 g/6 oz Vanilla Sugar, add 30 g/1 oz cocoa powder to make Chocolate Cigars.

Pepper Lime Ice Cream

First enigmatic, then addictive, these flavours tease and refresh the palate. Cool down, then meltdown. Particularly spectacular on top of a purée of icy pink watermelon.

440 g/14 oz caster sugar

6 to 8 large limes

1 litre/32 fl oz buttermilk

Put the sugar in a medium-size bowl. Grate enough of the lime rinds to make 1½ tablespoons lime zest. Juice as many limes as needed to get 125 ml/4 fl oz lime juice. Add zest and juice to sugar in bowl and mix well.

Add the buttermilk, ⅛ teaspoon salt and 1 tablespoon coarse ground black pepper. Stir until the sugar is dissolved.

Chill 4 hours or overnight, then freeze in an ice-cream maker according to manufacturer's instructions. Serve in ice-cream dishes or in lime shells.

Makes 1.5 litres/2½ pints, serving 8

ADD-ONS

Splash with tequila. Serve in soup plates on top of a puddle of chilled puréed watermelon or on a mound of diced mango.

Fresh Berry "Kir Imperial"

Nothing beats the simplicity and beauty of this drink-qua-dessert. Use tall champagne flutes and pile high with berries and bubbles. Use a good-quality demi-sec champagne or sparkling wine.

> **500 g/1 lb fresh ripe raspberries—plus more for garnish (optional)**
>
> **1 bottle sparkling wine or champagne, chilled**
>
> **375 g/12 oz fresh blueberries—plus more for garnish (optional)**

Put 8 champagne flutes in the freezer.

Put half of the raspberries and 6 tablespoons of the champagne in a blender and purée until very smooth.

Remove the glasses from the freezer. In each glass, put 3 tablespoons of raspberries and 3 tablespoons blueberries and pour some raspberry purée over the berries. Fill the glass to the top with champagne. Garnish with extra berries, if desired.

Serves 8

ADD-ONS

Garnish with fresh mint. Serve with Vanilla Sugar "Cigars" (page 255).

Little Lemons Filled with Lemon Yogurt "Gelato"

ADD-ONS

Garnish with sprigs of
fresh lemon balm or
lemon leaves.

*This exhilarating yet simple dessert is dedicated to Trattoria da Paolino,
also known as The Lemon Tree, in Capri, where one dines outdoors in a
perfumed lemon grove . . . in a cool breeze.*

> 10 large lemons: 6 whole lemons; grated zest of
> 2 lemons; 150 ml/5 fl oz freshly squeezed
> lemon juice
>
> 185 g/6 oz sugar
>
> 375 g/12 oz natural yogurt

Combine the lemon juice, sugar, lemon zest and ⅛ teaspoon coarse
salt in a nonreactive bowl. Stir well until the sugar dissolves. Whisk in
the yogurt and blend thoroughly. Chill overnight.

Cut a 8-mm/⅓-inch "hat" off the tops of lemons, saving the tops.
With a paring knife, cut out most of pulp from each lemon and then,
with a spoon, scrape the remaining pulp from the sides. Turn the
lemons upside down on kitchen paper to drain. If necessary, cut small
slices off lemon bottoms so they can stand firmly.

Meanwhile, pour the yogurt mixture into an ice-cream maker and
prepare according to the manufacturer's instructions.

Fill each lemon shell with ice cream, mounding it 12 mm/½ inch
over the top of the shell, and cover with the lemon "hat." Freeze until hard. Let sit at room temperature 10 to 15 minutes before serving.

Serves 6

Chocolate Truffle Torte

Pure gourmandise. This style of cake also has been known affectionately as "Chocolate Decadence," "Death by Chocolate," "Aunt Sonia's Chocolate Problem," and other such hedonistic names—all of which apply.

> 750 g/1½ lb good-quality dark chocolate
> (Valrhona, if possible)
>
> 30 g/1 oz unsalted butter
>
> 375 ml/12 fl oz double cream—plus 125 ml/
> 4 fl oz additional to be whipped for topping
> (optional)

Chop chocolate into small chunks and melt in the top of a double boiler over simmering water. Do not allow the chocolate to get too hot or it will seize up and become hard and dry. When the mixture is melted, remove it from the heat, put it in the bowl of an electric mixer and whip with the butter and 375 ml/12 fl oz of the cream until all the ingredients are well incorporated.

Line the bottom of a 23-cm/9-inch springform tin with grease-proof paper and pour the chocolate mixture into the tin. Let cool. Cover and chill for at least 8 hours.

Before serving, run the blade of a sharp knife around the edge of the cake to loosen it. Remove from the tin. Cut with a knife that has been dipped in hot water. If desired, whip the additional double cream and serve with cake.

Serves 12 to 16

ADD-ONS

Add several table-spoons of grappa to the melted chocolate. Dust the cake with cocoa, or top it with fresh raspberries before chilling.

GRAPENOTE

An unexpected treat is a glass of lightly chilled Banyuls, a sweet red wine made from grenache; try one from Domaine de la Rectorie. Or serve a ruby port.

"Cannoli" Custard

Clemenza, in the film The Godfather, *says, "Leave the gun. Take the cannolis." I say, keep the custard. Who needs the shells?*

500 g/1 lb low-fat ricotta cheese

9 tablespoons icing sugar

¾ teaspoon rum essence

Gently whip the ricotta, sugar and rum essence in the bowl of an electric mixer. Do not overblend. Divide equally among 3 or 4 martini glasses. Chill well. Sprinkle additional icing sugar, through a coarse sieve, over the top of the custard just before serving.

Serves 4

ADD-ONS

Fold in 60 g/2 oz miniature chocolate drops or white raisins plumped in rum. Sprinkle crushed amaretti biscuits or grated chocolate on top.

GRAPENOTES

Serve with ice-cold shots of Strega. Follow with a very short espresso.

Strawberry Summer Pudding

Invented for the peak-of-season berry dessert, my all-strawberry version relies on seasonally correct, ripe, red fruit bursting with juices and perfume. If you have the pleasure of picking your own from a local strawberry farm, select the ripest—even overripe berries—and rush home to make this dessert.

> 1 kg/2 lb very ripe strawberries
>
> 315 g/10 oz sugar
>
> 1 (500-g/1-lb) loaf good-quality sliced white bread

Reserve eight of the strawberries for a garnish and hull the remaining strawberries. Wash them in a colander and drain well. Transfer a third of the hulled strawberries to a large flat-bottomed pan. Add the sugar and mash gently with a potato masher, leaving large pieces. Cut the remaining hulled berries in half. Add them to the pan, cook over high heat for 30 seconds, let cool and reserve.

Cut the crusts from the bread slices. Line the bottom and sides of 2-litre/64-fl oz basin with bread, cutting the bread so the bowl is covered completely, leaving no gaps. Spoon the berries and juices into the bread-lined basin. Cover the top completely with more bread, again leaving no spaces. Select a plate that fits inside the bowl and place the plate on top of the bread. Put a weight on top of the plate, then wrap well with foil. Refrigerate for 8 to 12 hours.

Just before serving, invert onto a large decorative platter. Spoon any juices over the top of the pudding. Garnish with the reserved whole berries.

Serves 8

ADD-ONS

Serve with whipped double cream, crème fraîche or soured cream.

GRAPENOTE

How about a small shot of framboise?

Caramelized Pineapple, Black Pepper Syrup

Alchemy lesson: Start with an ordinary pineapple, poach it, and roast it, and you will have pineapple intensity of untold megabites. Add coarse ground pepper for a little "black magic."

1 large ripe pineapple (about 1.75 kg/3½ lb)

250 g/8 oz sugar

500 ml/16 fl oz good-quality vanilla ice cream

With a sharp knife, cut the skin off the pineapple, then cut the pineapple into six wedges. Remove the tough core.

Bring 1 litre/32 fl oz water and 185 g/6 oz of the sugar to a boil in a medium-size pan. Add the pineapple. Add enough water to cover the pineapple, if necessary. Lower the heat and cook 20 minutes, or until pineapple is tender but not too soft.

Remove the pineapple with tongs to a large squat glass jar or bowl. Reduce the syrup to 500 ml/16 fl oz. Pour through a sieve over the pineapple. Let marinate overnight.

Remove the pineapple from the poaching liquid. Reduce the poaching liquid to 250 ml/8 fl oz and add 1 teaspoon coarse ground black pepper. Let cool.

Place the pineapple on a baking tray and sprinkle heavily with the remaining sugar. Grill until the pineapple begins to caramelize. Turn the pineapple and grill on each side for 1 minute.

Put the pineapple on dessert plates. Serve with vanilla ice cream and poaching liquid.

Serves 6

Poires Belle-Hélène, Pear Sorbet

Even the august chef Escoffier proclaimed, Faîtes simple: *something akin to "Keep it simple, stupid." Although he didn't actually subscribe to 1-2-3, I think he would have loved this simple preparation of his classic coupling of poached pears and chocolate sauce—named, no doubt, after the famous operetta by Offenbach.*

10 large pears, 6 with long stems

500 g/1 lb granulated sugar

**180 ml/6 fl oz Chocolate Maple Syrup
(page 228)**

(page 228)

Carefully remove the skin from the 6 pears with long stems. Core from the bottom. Place the pears in a large heavy pan with water to cover. Add 125 g/4 oz sugar. Bring to a boil. Lower the heat, cover the pan and poach the pears for 20 to 30 minutes, until just tender. Let cool in liquid. Chill until very cold. Reserve 125 ml/4 fl oz cooking liquid.

Meanwhile, peel the remaining pears and cut into large chunks. Remove the core and any seeds. Put in a pan with 500 ml/16 fl oz water and 375 g/12 oz sugar. Cook until very soft; cooking time will vary depending on the pear. Purée in a food processor with the reserved cooking liquid. Process until smooth. Chill several hours. Put mixture in ice-cream maker and make sorbet according to the manufacturer's instructions.

To serve, place a scoop of sorbet in a large goblet, top with a whole pear and spoon chocolate sauce over the pear. Serve immediately.

Serves 6

Garnish with candied violets.

GRAPENOTES

Accompany with a glass of Poire William, straight from the freezer.

Pumpkin Pavé

Pavé means "slab," or "block," in French. This pavé tastes suspiciously like an American Thanksgiving pie. It's very elegant when sliced and served with rosettes of whipped cream or drizzled with Chocolate Maple Syrup (page 228).

ADD-ONS

Put Chocolate Maple Syrup (page 228) in a squeeze bottle and drizzle over pavé.

5 extra-large eggs

940 g/30 oz tinned pumpkin pie filling

250 ml/8 fl oz double cream

Preheat the oven to 180°C/350°F/gas 4.

In the bowl of an electric mixer, beat the eggs with pinch of salt until well blended. Add the pumpkin pie filling and mix until very smooth. Slowly add the double cream and continue to mix until smooth and creamy.

Pour the mixture into a nonstick 24- by 14-cm/9½- by 5½-inch loaf tin. Bake in a water bath for 1½ hours.

Remove from the water bath and let cool, then refrigerate 3 or 4 hours.

Slice and place on chilled dessert plates. If desired, whip some additional double cream and serve the pavé with a dollop.

Serves 12

Yogurt "Coeur à la Crème," Apricot Compote

My inspiration came from a classic Turkish dessert of thickened yogurt sandwiched between poached apricot halves. But my results bear a striking resemblance to the classic coeur à la crème, *a rich cream-cheese dessert made in a heart-shaped mould. This ultra-rich-tasting dessert has no fat!*

500 g/1 lb large dried apricots

1.25 litres/2 pints fat-free vanilla yogurt

60 ml/2 fl oz Tuaca liqueur (or any other orange-flavoured liqueur)—plus more for drizzling if desired

Soak the apricots in 750 ml/24 fl oz of water overnight.

Line a 19-cm/7½-inch coarse mesh sieve with several layers of muslin. Put the yogurt in the sieve and place over a bowl to catch drippings. Press down on the yogurt a few times to help release any liquid. Let drain 5 to 6 hours. The yogurt will become very dense and thick, turning into what is now called yogurt cheese.

Meanwhile, cook the apricots and soaking liquid in a covered pan over medium heat for 20 minutes. Mash lightly and add the 60 ml/ 2 fl oz liqueur. Cook 1 to 2 minutes, long enough to let most of the liquid evaporate but leaving the apricots juicy, not dry.

To serve, place all but 1 or 2 of the chilled apricots on a large round decorative tray or platter. Turn out yogurt cheese onto apricots. Slice the remaining apricots and use them to garnish the top. Cover with cling film and chill until ready to serve. Sprinkle with additional liqueur if desired.

Serves 6

ADD-ONS

Garnish with chopped pistachio nuts or fresh mint.

GRAPENOTE

Remarkable with a glass of Hungarian Tokay with 4 to 6 "puttonyos," which signify the degrees of sweetness.

Mille-feuille of Roquefort and Sauternes

ADD-ONS

Before serving, dust the top with 1 tablespoon icing sugar passed through a sieve or doily. You can add thinly sliced peeled pears to layers in mille-feuille or serve with grapes and walnuts. For a great little meal, accompany with Wild Greens and Blood Orange Salad, Orange Vinaigrette (page 75).

GRAPENOTE

Serve a glass of costly-but-worth-it chilled Sauternes: Château d'Yquem or slightly more modest Château Climens.

A sophisticated dessert for those who don't love sweets. This delectable mille-feuille layered with incomparable flavours of Roquefort and Sauternes, will leave you feeling richly rewarded, especially when it's served with a small glass of chilled Sauternes. Château d'Yquem, anyone?

1 sheet frozen puff pastry, defrosted (about 250 g/8 oz)

155 to 185 g/5 to 6 oz Roquefort cheese, at room temperature

60 ml/2 fl oz Sauternes

Preheat the oven to 190°C/375°F/gas 5.

Roll out the pastry to make a 23- by 23-cm/9- by 9-inch square. Cut in half, put one piece on top of the other (you will have a rectangle), and press lightly. Bake 20 minutes, or until golden brown. Remove from oven.

Mix the cheese and the Sauternes in food processor until smooth. Cut the pastry horizontally into 3 equal layers. Spread half the cheese mixture on the bottom layer. Top with the second sheet of pastry and repeat. Cover with the third piece of pastry and press lightly. Refrigerate for several hours. When ready to serve, let mille-feuille come to room temperature.

Serves 8

Snitz Pie

A good apple pie goes a long way to assuring domestic tranquillity. No one will ever know that this pie begins with snitz—what the Pennsylvania Dutch call dried apples—but everyone will be happy.

> **250 g/8 oz dried apple slices**
>
> **125 g/4 oz plus 1 tablespoon Vanilla Sugar (page 224)**
>
> **Pastry for a 23-cm/9-inch pie, top and bottom (see Note)**

Soak apples overnight in 750 ml/24 fl oz water. Cook in soaking water, covered, for 20 minutes, or until apples are very soft. Mash coarsely in a pan, using a wooden spoon. Cook 1 minute to let all water evaporate. Add the 125 g/4 oz vanilla sugar, mix well and cook another minute. Let cool.

Preheat the oven to 220°C/425°F/gas 7.

Turn apple mixture into a pastry-lined tin, cover with the top piece of pastry and crimp the pastry together. Make 2 or 3 slits to let the steam escape. Sprinkle with the 1 tablespoon remaining sugar.

Bake for 10 minutes. Reduce heat to 180°C/350°F/gas 4 and bake 30 minutes longer. Let cool completely before serving.

Serves 8

Note: You can use a good-quality bought pastry or make your own (page 268).

ADD-ONS

Add ¼ teaspoon ground allspice to the mashed apples. Or serve with a small piece of sharp white cheddar cheese.

GRAPENOTE

How a about a snifter of Calvados to go with your coffee?

Flaky Pastry
for a 23-cm/9-inch pie

315 g/10 oz flour
105 g/3½ oz unsalted butter, cold, cut into small pieces
2 teaspoons sugar

Place the flour, butter and sugar and ½ teaspoon salt in a food processor and process until the mixture resembles coarse crumbs, about 10 seconds. Add 7 to 8 tablespoons iced water and pulse until the pastry begins to hold together.

Turn the pastry out onto greaseproof paper and flatten the dough into a circle. Add a little flour if dough is sticky. Wrap in greaseproof paper and refrigerate 1 hour.

Cut the dough into two pieces, making one piece a little larger than the other. The larger piece will be for the bottom of the pie. At this point, you can freeze this dough for future use or proceed to make a pie.

On a lightly floured surface, roll out the larger piece and fit it into a 23-cm/9-inch flan tin. Fill the pie. Roll out the smaller piece to a dimension large enough to cover the filling. Fold in half for easy handling and place on top of pie. Unfold and fit the top pastry piece onto the base pastry. Crimp the edges together and you're ready for baking.

Almond Brittle from Sicily

With these basic ingredients, you can always make confectionery for guests while filling your house with inviting aromas. This confection, known in Sicily as torrone di mandorle, *is truly authentic when made with almonds, but here you can use peanuts if you like.*

500 g/1 lb sugar

500 g/1 lb shelled almonds or peanuts

½ lemon

In a large, heavy nonstick frying pan or saucepan, heat the sugar and almonds over a very low flame, stirring constantly. The sugar will colour slowly and crystallize around the almonds. This will take about 20 minutes.

The torrone is ready to be poured when the sugar is completely melted and a dark-brown colour. Should the sugar lumps form, be patient; they will dissolve if kept over a very low flame for 5 more minutes. Be careful not to let it burn.

Turn out onto a marble surface. Very carefully flatten into a thin sheet using the cut side of the lemon half. The mixture is very hot, so keep your fingers clear.

Let cool. Break into pieces using a hammer and a heavy knife.

Makes about 1 kg/2 lb

Mixed Fruit Rumtopf

ADD-ONS

Serve with double
cream or crème
fraîche. Nice also with
Sweet Zwieback
(page 271).

Desserts for winter need to be lusty and comforting. Often we want some-
thing warm, or something showy enough to serve guests during the
Christmas season, so learn to flambé and add razzle-dazzle to this
drunken fruit compote. The biscotti-like biscuits are perfect for dunking.

500 g/1 lb mixed dried fruit

250 ml/8 fl oz dark rum

125 g/4 oz sugar

Put the dried fruit, rum and sugar in a large jar with a cover. Add
water to cover—600 ml/1 pint to 750 ml/24 fl oz. Cover and shake to
help sugar dissolve.

Let sit for a minimum of three days in a cool, dark place, periodically adding water to barely cover. If storing longer, add rum from
time to time to cover fruit. This gets even more delicious after one
month.

When ready to serve, remove the fruit with a slotted spoon and cut
into smaller pieces, if desired. Serve in goblets with liquid. Serve cold
or warm. Flambé with rum if desired.

Serves 6 to 8

Sweet Zwieback

This simple little twice-baked biscuit is somewhere between Jewish mandelbrot and Italian biscotti. Great for dunking, great for teething.

2 eggs

155 g/5 oz Vanilla Sugar (page 224)

155 g/5 oz flour

Preheat the oven to 200°C/400°F/gas 6.

Beat the eggs with a pinch of salt in an electric mixer for 5 to 6 minutes, until very thick and creamy. Add the vanilla sugar and beat 1 more minute. Lower speed and gradually add the flour.

Pour the batter into a nonstick 20-cm/8-inch loaf tin. Bake 25 to 30 minutes (or until a cocktail stick comes out dry). Remove from the oven and let cool in the pan on a wire rack.

Lower the oven temperature to 135°C/ 275°F/gas 1.

Remove the loaf from the tin and slice into sixteen 6-mm/¼-inch-thick slices. Put the slices on a baking tray and bake 8 to 10 minutes on each side—until they just begin to colour. Remove from the oven and let cool on a wire rack.

Makes 16 biscuits

ADD-ONS

Add 1 teaspoon anise seed to the batter.

GRAPENOTE

Wonderful for dunking into Vin Santo.

Spoonbread Pain Perdu

ADD-ONS

This is lovely served
with Strawberry
Spoon Fruit
(opposite) instead
of maple syrup.

It's worth making a double portion of spoonbread custard to have enough for leftovers. This crisp and creamy preparation doubles as a dessert or a very tasty dish for brunch. Pain perdu *means "lost bread" and has become synonymous with French toast.*

½ recipe for Spoonbread Custard (page 188)
(leftover is fine)

30 g/1 oz unsalted butter

125 ml/4 fl oz pure maple syrup

Cut the spoonbread custard into thick triangles. Melt the butter in a medium-size nonstick frying pan with a cover. Sauté the spoonbread custard on each side for 1 or 2 minutes until crispy.

Cover the frying pan and cook for 5 minutes over medium heat. The spoonbread custard will be hot and creamy on the inside, crisp on the outside. Serve with maple syrup.

Serves 3 to 4

Strawberry Spoon Fruit

500 g/1 lb fully ripe fresh strawberries
315 g/10 oz sugar
1 tablespoon fresh lemon juice

Wash and hull the berries. Cut large berries in quarters and smaller ones in half.

In a medium-size enamel pan, alternate layers of berries and sugar. Bring to a boil, then cook over medium-high heat for 20 minutes.

With a slotted spoon, remove the fruit to a jar. Add lemon juice to the juices in the pan and boil over high heat for 10 minutes, until the juices are reduced by half and are thick and syrupy. Pour the syrup over the berries. Let cool, then refrigerate.

Makes 500 ml/16 fl oz

Sliced Lemon Pie

This unlikely pie might inspire some controversy, since the lemons melt into a puckery, tart jelly. I enjoy its clean flavours immensely, especially with a cup of tea. You'll either love it or leave it.

ADD-ONS

Scatter a dozen leaves of fresh tarragon on lemons before affixing top crust. Serve with whipped cream.

4 medium-size lemons (about 375 g/12 oz)

pastry for 23-cm/9-inch pie, top and bottom (see Note)

250 g/8 oz Vanilla Sugar (page 224)

Preheat the oven to 150°C/300°F/gas 2.

Peel the lemons using a sharp knife, making sure white pith is completely removed. Slice lemons 3 mm/⅛ inch thick. Remove any seeds.

Line a 23-cm/9-inch flan tin with the pastry. Put the sugar in the pastry case in an even layer. Cover evenly with the lemon slices. Place the upper pastry on top of the sliced lemons, pressing the edges very tightly to seal them.

Place the pie on a baking tray and bake 1 hour.

Let cool completely before serving.

Serves 8 to 10

Note: You can use a good-quality bought pastry or make your own (page 268).

Granola Fruit Cobbler

Ripe, juicy fruit is fundamental to this homey cobbler, also known as a crisp, crunch or grunt. The more aromatic the fruit, the more luscious the results.

ADD-ONS

Serve with butter-pecan ice cream.

1 kg/2 lb very ripe stonefruit: nectarines, peaches, or plums

500 g/1 lb crunchy oat cereal (granola)

75 g/2½ oz unsalted butter, at room temperature

Preheat the oven to 165°C/325°F/gas 3.

Peel the fruit and slice into 12-mm/½-inch-thick wedges. Set aside.

Put half of the cereal in the bowl of a food processor. Process until the cereal is like coarse flour. Add 60 g/2 oz of the butter and process until the mixture becomes a sticky ball.

Put the dough in a bowl and add the remaining cereal and a pinch of salt. Mix well with your hands until the mixture is crumbly.

Put the sliced fruit and 3 tablespoons water in a 1.5-litre/2½-pint soufflé dish or other ovenproof dish and dot with the remaining butter. Pack the cereal mixture on top of the fruit to cover completely.

Bake 30 minutes. Serve warm but not right out of oven—let it sit at least 20 minutes. It's also good at room temperature.

Serves 6

Amaretto "Creamsicle" in Frozen Oranges

Frosty orange water ice enrobing vanilla ice cream is a taste memory of my childhood—a time of innocence before anyone knew the word "sorbet." With an adult splash of amaretto, flavours intensify into a seductive new dessert.

> 1 litre/32 fl oz mixed vanilla ice cream and orange sorbet
>
> 125 ml/4 fl oz amaretto
>
> 8 navel oranges

Let the ice cream and sorbet soften slightly. Put in the bowl of an electric mixer or a food processor with 60 ml/2 fl oz of the amaretto. Mix until smooth. Work quickly so the ice cream doesn't get soupy. Place the mixture in the freezer.

Cut a 12-mm/½-inch hat off the tops of 6 oranges. Scoop out the centres of the oranges, leaving 2.5-cm/1 inch on the bottom. Fill the oranges high with the ice-cream mixture and place the hats on top. Refreeze.

Peel the remaining 2 oranges and cut them into segments between membranes, removing all the membrane. Put them in a bowl with the remaining amaretto. Serve as a garnish for the frozen oranges.

Serves 6

Grapefruit in Campari Syrup, Crystallized Grapefruit

Crystallizing grapefruit rind is a bit labour-intensive, and you don't need to do it; this refreshing dessert has its own charm. If you do make the effort to transform bitter citrus skin into this delectable confection, however, the results will be spectacular.

> **5 very large grapefruit**
>
> **90g/3 oz plus 60 g/2 oz sugar**
>
> **2 tablespoons Campari**

Remove the rind of 2 grapefruit with a vegetable peeler and reserve.

Cut the skins completely off all the grapefruit, exposing the flesh. Remove all the white pith with a sharp knife. Cut between membranes to separate segments, removing all the membrane. Put in a bowl.

Collect all the juice and place it in a small pan with the 80 ml/3 fl oz sugar, 250 ml/8 fl oz water and the Campari. Simmer for 15 minutes, or until the syrup is reduced to 180 ml/6 fl oz. Pour the syrup through a sieve over the grapefruit segments. Refrigerate until very cold.

Cut the pith from the reserved grapefruit rind and cut the rind into thin julienne strips 5 cm/2 inches long. Place in a small saucepan, cover with water, and boil 20 minutes. Repeat the process two more times, discarding the cooking water each time. After cooking, put the rind and the 60 g/2 oz sugar in the saucepan. Let simmer a few minutes until the sugar is incorporated and the skins are clear. Let cool.

To serve, place the grapefruit segments in overlapping circular fashion on dessert plates or in flat soup plates. Pour several tablespoons of syrup over each and garnish with a mound of crystallized grapefruit.

Serves 6

Pots de Crème:
Chocolat et Vanille

Decidedly French, pots de crème *refer simultaneously to little lidded cups and to the heavenly custard within. I like to serve two per guest—one vanilla, one chocolate—and to think about Paris in the twenties.*

Au Chocolat

500 ml/16 fl oz double cream

125 g/4 oz good-quality dark chocolate, melted

3 egg yolks

Preheat the oven to 165°C/325°F/gas 3.

Heat the cream in a double boiler over simmering water. Add the chocolate and a pinch of salt and stir until mixture is blended.

Beat the egg yolks until light and lemon-coloured and pour the hot cream over them, a little at a time, whisking constantly.

Pour the mixture into crème pots, small ramekins or espresso cups. The shape and thickness of the container you use for baking will affect the timing. Cover with crème-pot covers or foil. Place the pots in a deep baking tin on the middle shelf. Pour enough hot water into the tin to come halfway up the side of the pots.

Bake until the centre is set (barely jiggles when shaken), from 15 to 20 minutes. Remove from the water bath and let cool. Chill well.

A la Vanille

6 egg yolks

125 g/4 oz Vanilla Sugar (page 224)

500 ml/16 fl oz single cream

Preheat the oven to 165°C/325°F/gas 3.

Beat the yolks until light and lemon-coloured. Gradually beat in the vanilla sugar and a pinch of salt. Add 60 ml/2 fl oz of the cream.

Scald the remaining cream and gradually stir into the mixture. You will have about 750 ml/24 fl oz.

Strain through a fine sieve into crème pots, small ramekins or espresso cups. The shape and thickness of the container you use for baking will affect the timing. Cover with crème-pot covers or foil. Place the pots in a deep baking tin on the middle shelf. Pour enough hot water into the tin to come halfway up the side of the pots.

Bake until the centre is set (barely jiggles when shaken), about 35 minutes. Remove from the water bath and let cool. Chill well.

Each flavour makes 6 servings

Chutney-Baked Apples,
Vanilla Cream

ADD-ONS

Cover the tops of the apples with lightly toasted sliced almonds after baking.

An unexpected chutney filling brings out all the qualities you want in a baked apple: syrupy sweetness, good acidity, aromatic spices, an occasional raisin.

As for the cream, is there any way to improve on a tub of melted Häagen Dazs vanilla?

6 large Red Delicious or Rome apples

180 ml/6 fl oz mango chutney (Major Grey's)

500 ml/16 fl oz super-premium vanilla ice cream

Preheat the oven to 200°C/400°F/gas 6.

Cut 6 mm/¼ inch off the top of the apples. Core the apples, being careful not to cut through the bottom. Fill cavity with chutney and cover tops with a thin layer of chutney syrup.

Place in a baking tin with 12 mm/½ inch of water. Bake 45 to 50 minutes, until the apples are soft but not falling apart.

Meanwhile, let the ice cream come to room temperature until it melts completely.

Remove the apples from the oven. Let them cool 15 to 20 minutes. Place in soup plates and pour vanilla "cream" around base of apples.

Serves 6

Frozen Hot Chocolate

I fondly recall this dessert, made famous at New York's Serendipity, where sophisticates celebrated their birthdays before they became sophisticated. The portion was huge, the chocolate slush numbed your mouth—what unforgettable fun! Keep a trayful in your freezer for "spontaneous consumption."

> **60 g/2 oz cocoa powder**
>
> **185 g/6 oz sugar**
>
> **600 ml/1 pint milk**

Put the cocoa and sugar in a medium-size enamel saucepan. Add 125 ml/4 fl oz of the milk to form a smooth paste. Slowly add the remaining milk and simmer until sugar dissolves and mixture is smooth. Let cool.

Pour the mixture into metal ice cube trays (it may stick to plastic) and freeze a minimum of 8 hours. Remove from trays and break up the frozen cubes with a fork.

Leave the food processor bowl fitted with a steel blade in the freezer for 1 hour. Then put in the broken-up cubes and 2 tablespoons water and process until smooth. Serve immediately in frozen coffee cups or goblets.

Serves 4 to 6

Add-Ons

Serve with a dollop of sweetened whipped cream and a dusting of cocoa powder. Tuck in a cinnamon stick or serve with warm Cinnamon Croûtes (page 282).

Grapenote

Very adult with a soupçon of coffee-flavoured liqueur, such as Tía María.

Cinnamon Croûtes

6 slices good-quality white bread
45 g/1½ oz apple butter
2 tablespoons Cinnamon Sugar (page 224)

Remove the crusts from the bread with sharp knife. Cut two 7.5-cm/ 1½-inch round croûtes from each slice of bread with a biscuit cutter. Brush one side completely with apple butter. Sprinkle with cinnamon sugar. Toast in oven until sugar melts.

Makes 12 croûtes

Hazelnut Tea Cake

Here's an easy way to have your cake and then eat it, for just when you think there's nothing to go with a cup of coffee, you can whip (literally) three simple ingredients into a lovely cake with a delicate crumb.

250 g/8 oz hazelnuts with skins

2 extra-large eggs

125 ml/4 fl oz pure maple syrup, plus 1 or 2 tablespoons for glaze

Preheat the oven to 180°C/350°F/gas 4.

Toast the nuts in a nonstick frying pan until you just begin to smell a faint nutty aroma. Let cool.

Put the eggs and syrup in a large warmed bowl. Add a pinch of salt and beat with an electric mixer at medium-high speed for 6 or 7 minutes, until the mixture has increased substantially in volume.

Grind the nuts finely in a food processor until powdery and mix into the egg mixture. Pour into a nonstick 21-cm/8½-inch loaf tin lined with greaseproof paper on the bottom.

Bake 35 to 40 minutes, or until a cocktail stick inserted in the cake comes out clean. Glaze with 1 or 2 tablespoons maple syrup, spread with a pastry brush. Let cool.

Serves 8 to 10

ADD-ONS

Add grated zest of 1 orange to batter.

GRAPENOTE

Nice with sweet sherry such as Emilio Lustau's Pedro Ximinez Reserve, or orange-scented "Essencia" from Quady, in California.

Turkish Cherry Bread

ADD-ONS

Add 2 tablespoons brandy to cherries while cooking.

This unusual dessert is a sight to behold and lovely to eat. Fresh ruby cherries, gently poached, sit proudly on top of a cinnamon-raisin sponge, soaking up glistening juices. Evanescent at best, the cherry season is short but sweet.

625 g/1¼ lb fresh ripe cherries

155 g/5 oz sugar

8 slices cinnamon-raisin bread

Stone the cherries, leaving as many whole as you can, or use a cherry stoner. If the cherries are ripe, it's easy to do this with your fingers.

Put the cherries in a nonreactive pan with the sugar. Let sit 30 minutes.

Meanwhile, put 2 slices of bread together and trim the crusts, making perfect squares. Repeat until you have 4 bread stacks. Toast the stacks well in the oven until browned and crisped on both sides. Place on a platter.

Add 80 ml/3 fl oz water to the cherries and cook over medium-high heat for 15 minutes until soft. Pour the hot cherries and syrup evenly over the bread. Let cool.

Serves 4

Strawberries and Candied Ginger Dipped in Chocolate

Elemental flavours, basic and powerful. Have a bite of strawberry, then one of ginger then strawberry. Continue until you have satisfied your craving.

185 g/6 oz good-quality bittersweet or plain chocolate, chopped

16 large ripe strawberries with long stems

16 large pieces of candied ginger

In the top of a double boiler set over hot water, melt the chocolate, stirring occasionally. Remove the chocolate from the heat and keep it over hot water to prevent it becoming too thick.

Holding each strawberry by the stem, dip it into the chocolate, coating two-thirds of the berry. Let any excess drip off. Put the strawberries on a baking tray lined with foil or greaseproof paper. Chill until hardened.

Pierce each piece of ginger with a cocktail stick and dip it into the chocolate to coat two-thirds, letting excess drip off. Place on a tray until hardened.

Makes 32 pieces

ADD-ONS

You can add 2 tablespoons unsalted butter or vegetable lard to the melted chocolate for a shinier appearance. When the chocolate has set, you can "double-dip" strawberries and ginger in melted white chocolate, leaving a band of dark chocolate exposed.

Cranberry Chutney

Light brown sugar provides moderate sweetness against a backdrop of ultra-tart cranberries. It is, after all, the sweet-and-sour synergy that makes chutney chutney! Bits of candied ginger provide zings of intense flavour. This chutney ages well in your fridge.

500 g/1 lb cranberries

155 g/5 oz light soft brown sugar

2 tablespoons very finely minced candied ginger

Put the cranberries, sugar, ginger and 150 ml/5 fl oz water in a heavy, medium-size pan. Bring to a boil, lower the heat, add a pinch of salt and a pinch of freshly ground black pepper and cook over medium heat for 8 to 10 minutes, until cranberries have popped and sauce has thickened. Chill well.

Makes about 600 ml/1 pint

Red Wine Apple Sauce

Often, a sweet grace note is desired alongside a festive roast turkey, duck or goose. For an alternative, this apple sauce also would cozy up smartly to a bold pot roast (page 168) and a crisp French Potato Cake (page 207).

6 large tart apples (about 1.25 kg/2½ lb)

2 tablespoons Cinnamon Sugar (page 224)

150 ml/5 fl oz sweet red wine

Peel and core the apples and cut them into large wedges. Put the apples, cinnamon sugar and wine and some freshly ground black pepper in a medium-size nonreactive heavy pan with a cover. Bring to a boil, lower the heat, cover and cook 15 minutes. Uncover and cook 10 minutes longer, or until most of the liquid has evaporated.

Mash lightly with a potato masher, leaving some chunks of apple. Chill well. This apple sauce can be made 4 to 5 days ahead.

Makes 750 ml/24 fl oz

Fat-Free, Low-Fat, Low-Calorie Recipes

FAT-FREE RECIPES

Port Consommé
Fennel, Leek and Orzo Soup
"Fire and Ice" Gazpacho
Sauerkraut "Hangover" Soup
Curried Lentil Soup
Ginger Pepperpot, "Glass" Noodles
Pickled Greens
Cranberry Chutney
Herbes de Provence Vinegar
Labaneh (if made with fat-free yogurt)
Red Onion Salad
Red Wine Apple Sauce
Strawberries in Grappa
Pastel Easter Sorbet
Chianti Granita
Prune Jelly with Prune Kernels
Mixed Fruit Rumtopf
Fresh Berry "Kir Imperial"
Grapefruit in Campari Syrup, Crystallized
    Grapefruit
Yogurt "Coeur à la Crème," Apricot Compote
    (if made with fat free yogurt)
Iced Bedouin Coffee

LOW-FAT RECIPES

Party Food and Appetizers
5 grams of fat or less

Aubergine on Fire
Black Hummus
Tiny Pepper Cheese Crackers (1)
Med-Rim Lamb Nuggets
Angels and Archangels on Horseback
Fried Chickpeas with Sage and Walnut Oil
    (60-ml/2-fl oz portion)
Rosettes of Smoked Salmon on Cucumber
    Rounds
Party Wraps: (1 wrap)
    Vine Leaves and Haloumi
    Radicchio and Smoked Mozzarella
Za'atar Pita (2 pieces)

First Courses
5 grams of fat or less

Celery Rémoulade, Celeriac Crisps
Swedish Cured Salmon (90-g/3-oz portion)

Soups
5 grams of fat or less

Yellow Turnip Soubise
Chilled Cauliflower Crème
Soupy Red Beans with Smoked Ham
An Unusual Borscht: Roast Beetroot, Squash
 and Yogurt
Yellow Pea and Bacon Potage

Main Courses
10 grams of fat or less

Tuna Burger, Hoisin and Pickled Ginger Root
Pepper-Seared Tuna, Cool Mango Relish
Roast Pork Tenderloin with Prunes and Bay
 Leaves

Vegetables and Side Dishes
5 grams of fat or less

Courgette, Black Olive and Tomato
 Compote
Turkish Pilaf with Tomato
White Polenta with Parmigiano-Reggiano
Potato-Fennel Mash
Broccoli di Rape I
Cumin-Scented Couscous
Orange and Gold Potato Purée, Sweet
 Potato Crisps
Barley-Buttermilk Salad
Wild Rice and Bulgur Toss
Aromatic Ginger Rice
Melted Tomatoes

Desserts
5 grams of fat or less

Orange Ambrosia
Little Lemons Filled with Lemon Yogurt
 "Gelato"
Turkish Cherry Bread
Strawberries and Candied Ginger Dipped in
 Chocolate (1 berry)
Lemon Buttermilk Ice Cream
Chocolate Milk Pudding
Oven-Roasted Strawberries, Fresh Strawberry
 Sorbet
Pepper Lime Ice Cream
Raspberry Cloud Soufflé

Miscellaneous
5 grams of fat or less

Beer Bread

LOW-CALORIE RECIPES

Party Food and Appetizers
Under 165 calories

Note: 30 g/1 oz of potato crisps have 150 calories.
Which would you rather have?

Cherry Tomato Bonbons
Black Hummus
Lemony Tahina
Aubergine on Fire
Za'atar Pita
Tiny Pepper Cheese Crackers (3)
Sherry Vinegar Mushrooms
Party Wraps:
 Vine Leaves and Haloumi (3 wraps)
 Radicchio and Smoked Mozzarella
  (2 wraps)
Fried Chickpeas with Sage and Walnut Oil

Rosettes of Smoked Salmon on Cucumber
  Rounds
Venetian Wafers
Med-Rim Lamb Nuggets
Angels and Archangels on Horseback
Ouzo Feta Spread (2 tablespoons)
Flying Saucers

First Courses
Under 165 Calories

Salmon Carpaccio Cooked on a Plate
Celery Rémoulade, Celeriac Crisps
Grilled Shiitake Mushrooms, Garlic Essence
Salad Frisée with Lardons and Hot Vinegar
  Dressing
Rocket and Mussel Salad, Anchovy
  Vinaigrette
Salad of Roast Beetroot and Beetroot Greens,
  Walnut Oil
Tomato, Mozzarella and Basil: Six Styles (if
  mozzarella is 30 g/1 oz or less)
Swedish Cured Salmon (90 g/3 oz salmon)
Wild Greens and Blood Orange Salad,
  Orange Vinaigrette

Soups
Under 165 Calories

Port Consommé
Fennel, Leek and Orzo Soup
"Fire and Ice" Gazpacho
Yellow Turnip Soubise
Chilled Cauliflower Crème
Sauerkraut "Hangover" Soup
Soupy Red Beans with Smoked Ham
Curried Lentil Soup
An Unusual Borscht: Roast Beetroot, Squash
  and Yogurt
Yellow Pea and Bacon Potage
Ginger Pepper Pot, "Glass" Noodles

"Cream" of Spinach Soup
Avocado Velouté, Fino Sherry
Chicken Broth 1-2-3
Fournade with Egyptian Spices
Carrot-Ginger Velvet
Red Wine Onion Soup

Main Courses
Under 350 Calories

Farfalle with Broccoli, Broccoli-Butter Sauce
Steamed Clams in Thyme Butter
Steamed Halibut, Sweet Pepper Confetti
Rosemary-Infused Swordfish
Pan-Seared Tuna Niçoise, Tomato "Water"
Roast Pork Tenderloin with Prunes and Bay
  Leaves
Roast Cod with Red Pepper Purée
Salmon Baked in Vine Leaves
Tuna Burger, Hoisin and Pickled Ginger Root
Pepper-Seared Tuna, Cool Mango Relish
Two-Way Salmon and Courgettes
Yogurt Chicken with Blackened Onions
Michael's Perfect Roast Turkey with Lemon
  and Sage (185-g/6-oz portion)
Arista: Roast Loin of Pork with Rosemary and
  Garlic
Braised Veal Roast with Leeks and Rosé Wine
  (200-g/6¹/₂-oz portion)
Coffee and Vinegar Pot Roast (185-g/6-oz
  portion)

Vegetables and Side Dishes
Under 165 Calories

Winter Squash and Orange Purée
Turkish Pilaf with Tomato
Steamed Broccoli, Stir-Fried Pecans
White Polenta with Parmigiano-Reggiano
Sugar Snaps in Orange Butter
Broccoli di Rape I-II-III

Wild Rice and Bulgur Toss
Caramelized Chicory and Bacon
Spoonbread Custard
Braised Celery Batons, Fried Celery
    Leaves
French Potato Cake
Giant Glazed Onions, Balsamic Vinegar
Cumin-Scented Couscous
Courgette, Black Olive and Tomato
    Compote
Smothered Lettuce with Sumac
Potato-Fennel Mash
Barley-Buttermilk Salad
Wilted Cucumbers, Dill Butter
Watercress Purée
Yucca "Hash Browns" with Red Pepper
Pan-Grilled Radicchio, Fried Rosemary
Oven-Roasted Asparagus, Fried Capers

Desserts
Under 165 calories

Strawberries in Grappa
Pastel Easter Sorbet
Chianti Granita
Orange Ambrosia
Little Lemons Filled with Lemon Yogurt
    "Gelato"
Turkish Cherry Bread

Strawberries and Candied Ginger Dipped in
    Chocolate (2 berries)
Lemon Buttermilk Ice Cream
Prune Jelly with Prune Kernels
Chocolate Milk Pudding
Oven-Roasted Strawberries, Fresh Strawberry
    Sorbet
Pepper Lime Ice Cream
Mixed Fruit Rumtopf, Sweet Zwieback
Green Melon Zabaglione
Syrian Shortbread (1 piece)
Marsala Oranges with Toasted Pine Nuts
Vanilla-Sugar Cigars
Pumpkin Pavé

Miscellaneous

Beer Bread
Caraway Cheese Crisps
Twice-Baked Oatcakes
Iced Bedouin Coffee
Pickled Greens
Cranberry Chutney
Herbes de Provence Vinegar
Labaneh
Red Onion Salad
Melted Tomatoes
Red Wine Apple Sauce
Sweet Mustard Sauce

Index